BUFFALO BILL'S GREAT WILD WEST SHOW

BUFFALO BILL'S
GREAT
WILD WEST SHOW

★

by WALTER HAVIGHURST

Illustrated by JOHN C. WONSETLER

RANDOM HOUSE · NEW YORK

First Printing

CONTENTS

1
The Old Glory Blowout

Out on the plains of Nebraska, along the new tracks of the Union Pacific Railroad, straggled the town of North Platte. Twice a day trains came through on their long run to California, and sometimes a band of cowboys galloped in from the big ranches. Otherwise North Platte was a quiet place in its great circle of prairie.

But on the Fourth of July, 1882, the town crackled with noise and excitement. Everybody in Lincoln County was there, with horses tied to the wagon wheels under the dusty trees.

When the noon train came through, passengers pressed to the windows. They heard a clatter of hoofs and rattle of rifle fire. They saw a flag on a cottonwood pole and hundreds of people surrounding a trampled field. Across the ground an Indian and a cowboy raced on half-wild ponies, and horsemen pounded after a herd of buffalo.

On that Independence Day people were celebrating all over America. In the cities Congressmen were making speeches and troops were marching down Main Street. In country towns children were shooting firecrackers while women laid out a picnic dinner under the courthouse trees. But North Platte was having a different kind of celebration.

The plainsmen were celebrating in their own way. Their speech-making was the shrill *Yipee!* of the cowboys and the *Ki-yi-yow!* of the Indians. Pistol and rifle shots were their firecrackers. They had a big dinner under the cottonwoods, and then the hoofs were thudding again in riding and roping contests. They called it The Old Glory Blowout.

From the train windows people saw a stagecoach rumble onto the field and a tall horseman galloping beside it. He wore a big hat, a pointed beard, and long hair falling to his shoulders. He was North Platte's leading citizen. His name was William Frederick Cody, but everybody in Nebraska called him Buffalo Bill. The Old Glory Blowout was his idea, and the people loved it.

Buffalo Bill had a roomy, rambling house in North Platte called the "Welcome Wigwam." There he entertained his friends—eastern businessmen, western army officers, old comrades of the Pony Express and the railroad crews. He also owned "Scout's Rest Ranch," a big spread of prairie beyond the western edge of town.

In this summer of 1882 Buffalo Bill was just halfway through his eventful life. Behind him lay thirty-six years of daring and danger on the plains; ahead waited thirty-six years of fame as a western showman.

As a boy in Kansas he had ridden his pony over

miles of rolling prairie. As a youth he had traveled west with wagon trains and had carried the mail on the Pony Express. As a young man he had hunted buffalo for the railroad camps; he fought the Indians and rode as a scout for the army. He had guided eastern sportsmen on long buffalo hunts.

The West, still wild and free, fascinated all Americans in the years following the Civil War.

Even in Chicago and New York, Buffalo Bill was a familiar name. He had appeared there on the stage, enacting scenes from the Indian wars on the plains. Eastern audiences were thrilled by any portrayal of western life.

But now, at North Platte on the Fourth of July, Buffalo Bill was putting on a show for sheer pleasure. The Old Glory Blowout had all the reckless action of frontier life. Sharpshooting contests, broncobusting, cattle-roping, the whoops and cries and clatter—this was the Wild West itself.

The men on horseback were Buffalo Bill's friends. There was lean, leathery Major Frank North, a veteran army scout and buffalo hunter.

He and Buffalo Bill were ranch partners; they owned a big cattle spread on the Dismal River in the empty stretches of central Nebraska. Buck Taylor, a tall, rangy, hard-riding young cowboy who had come west from Massachusetts, was the top hand on the Dismal River Ranch. Soft-voiced, bowlegged Con Groner had been sheriff of Lincoln County. A dead shot with a pistol and an expert horseman, he had caught murderers, horse thieves and cattle rustlers. Once he chased notorious Jesse James out of Lincoln County.

All these men had ridden wild horses, roped wild cattle and hunted buffalo. But the West was changing. Herds of longhorn steers had been driven up from Texas to the central plains. Now ranchers were driving cattle where the buffalo had roamed. The plains Indians, outnumbered by white settlers, were living on reservation lands. Beside the old road of the Pony Express and the wagon trains, ran the twin rails of the Union Pacific.

The most excited spectator at the Old Glory Blowout was a twelve-year-old boy. Johnny Baker ran up and down the field, watching the horse

races, the shooting matches, the bucking broncos. He didn't miss a thing.

Johnny was a Nebraska boy, as native as an
Indian. His father, Lew Baker, a veteran wagon
driver, had settled at O'Fallon's Bluff on the
Platte River sixteen miles west of town. The
Platte, old-timers said, was a mile wide and an
inch deep—except in spring when the snows were
melting on the distant ranges. Its water came
from the Laramie Mountains in Wyoming and
the high Rockies in Colorado. Johnny Baker's
father knew that far western country.

Three times the Indians drove Lew Baker away
from O'Fallon's Bluff. After the third raid he
moved his family into North Platte and there
Johnny Baker grew up. When old wagonmen
came to talk with his father, Johnny heard about
the dangerous days of the Old West.

One of Lew Baker's friends was a big, deep-
voiced man with hair falling to his shoulders—
Buffalo Bill. His stories fascinated Johnny, and
the boy followed him like a dog. Buffalo Bill was
his hero, for life.

Once Buffalo Bill took Johnny on a sixty-five-mile buggy trip to his Dismal River Ranch. As they jolted over the prairie the big man pointed. "There's where the Pawnees use' to have their camp. . . . That white patch out there—see it, like a snowbank?—that's all buff'lo bones, left by the hide hunters. . . . That draw in there under the ridge—right there a party of Sioux ambushed a line of wagons."

Then Buffalo Bill's voice dropped. "It's all gone, boy. I first saw North Platte when I wasn't much older than you, traveling with a bull train to Utah. There was a fording place there; beyond it the trail swung north, then west again." He stared over the prairie. "Now the trail is grassed over and coyotes bark at the railroad trains."

The country was changing. But on this Fourth of July, with the Indians whooping after a shaggy buffalo and cowboys clinging to bucking horses, the West was wild again. Johnny Baker breathed the dusty smell of cattle and the tang of gunpowder. He wished the Old Glory Blowout would never end.

While shadows fell across the field, the ranchers hitched their teams to the wagons and headed home. The Indians and cowboys scattered. Under the long shadows the town was quiet again.

Johnny Baker stayed till the field was empty. Then he went slowly home, keeping the riders and ropers, the horses and cattle in a restless picture in his mind. He couldn't let them go.

In the summer dusk, while the evening train whistled across the prairie, a rider reined his horse under the dusty trees. It was Buffalo Bill, looking over the trampled field where for a few hours the Old West had lived again.

He stayed there while dusk deepened on the prairie and the summer stars grew bright. He was thinking about a big idea. In his mind was a picture of a traveling show—Indians, scouts and cowboys, horses, steers and buffalo. He would take the Wild West to the world.

2
Johnny Baker Follows
the Show

The next spring was a busy season at Buffalo Bill's place on the edge of North Platte. He called it Scout's Rest Ranch, but no one rested during those April days of 1883.

On the broad ground in front of the ranch house the Wild West Show was assembling. Cowboys drove longhorn steers from the open range. From a neighboring ranch Merrill Keith and his horsemen brought a herd of shaggy buffalo. Half-wild horses milled around in a log corral. Behind six black mules rumbled a battered stagecoach. An ox team plodded ahead of a "prairie schooner," the covered wagon of the old plains trails.

To organize the show Buffalo Bill had the help of other men. Dr. A. W. Carver advanced money and bought equipment. He became Buffalo Bill's partner. Gordon W. Lillie, better known as "Pawnee Bill," brought a band of Pawnee braves from Oklahoma. They pitched their wigwams beside the restless horse corral. Major Frank North took charge of the Indians, and Buck Taylor, "King of the Cowboys," kept an eye on his reckless young horsemen.

Day after day in fine spring weather they practiced their performance. Cowboys rode bucking horses and dashed across the field in bronco races. Painted and feathered Indians ambushed the covered wagon and enacted a holdup of the Deadwood Stage.

The stagecoach had come from the famous gold camp of Deadwood Gulch. For years it carried valuable mail between Deadwood and Cheyenne.

Many times it had been attacked by Indians and bandits. Now, with the bullet-scarred stage, Buffalo Bill was re-enacting a dramatic scene from western adventure.

Practice, practice, practice—that was the way to make a show out of half-wild animals and restless men. The Indians and cowboys could not understand each other; only Pawnee Bill and Major North spoke the Indian tongue. When an act went wrong they translated Buffalo Bill's orders to the Indians; then the whole troop raced through it again. The events must go off in order and in time —a whole sequence of pounding action in two short hours. Practice, practice, practice.

Every day Johnny Baker was there, wondering, watching, waiting for a chance to help. When Buffalo Bill swung down from the saddle, Johnny reached for the bridle. "I'll hold your horse." When the big man wanted fresh ammunition, Johnny was ready. "I'll go. I'll get it." He was always there.

One of the men in that busy outfit was Major John M. Burke, a friend of Buffalo Bill's from his stage shows in the East. Major Burke became

the Wild West's press agent, getting publicity
for the show in the newspapers. He was an eastern man, from Washington, D. C., but he had
adopted western life. He wore his hair long, like
Buffalo Bill, under a wide-brimmed hat. He loved
to talk to the Indians in sign language. He called
himself "Arizona John," though he had never
been west of Nebraska.

Early in May, Major Burke went ahead of
the show to Omaha. He filled the papers with
news of the Wild West Show and arranged
for its first public appearance at the Omaha Fair
Grounds.

In the middle of May the show held its last re-
hearsal. Then it was loaded onto a sixteen-car
train. Horses, cattle, buffalo, and elk were herded
into a string of slatted stock cars. Carts and wagons and the old Deadwood Stage were loaded onto
flatcars. Guns and ammunition, harness, saddles
and bridles, performers' tents and Indian tepees
went into a boxcar. There was a separate car for
food, cooking equipment and the big, folded
cook tent. Teamsters and laborers, Indians and
cowboys and managers filled a line of coaches. It

was the strangest train that had ever arrived in Omaha.

At the fair grounds they unloaded, herding the restless animals into strong new corrals. When the tents and wigwams were set up and the wagons were in place, the show grounds looked like an encampment on the plains.

Over the grandstand hung a big banner:

THE WILD WEST
Hon. W. F. Cody and Dr. A. W. Carver's
ROCKY MOUNTAIN AND PRAIRIE EXHIBITION

It showed a picture of rolling plains, with a stagecoach, a covered wagon and some mounted Indians pursuing a herd of buffalo.

The term "Honorable" was attached to Buffalo Bill's name because he had been elected, a few years past, to the Nebraska legislature. In all the publicity Major Burke surrounded the show with dignity. He represented it not as a circus but as a historical portrayal of frontier life. His posters read: "The Green Sward Our Carpet, Heaven's Azure Canopy Our Canvas. No Tinsel,

No Gilding. No Humbug! No Side Shows or Freaks." It was a western spectacle under the windy sky, as honest and dramatic as a bucking bronco.

When Buffalo Bill came out of his tent, a familiar face smiled up at him.

"Why—what are you doing here, Johnny?"

"I followed the show," Johnny Baker said.

"This is a busy outfit, dangerous too. No place for a boy. You'll have to go back home."

That evening they planned the final details of the show. Next day would come the first public performance.

In the morning, walking past the Indian tepees, Buffalo Bill saw a boy eating bread and bacon with the Pawnees around a smoldering fire.

"Johnny," he said, "where did you sleep last night?"

Johnny Baker looked up. "On the hay, in the horse corral."

"Have you got any money?"

"No, sir."

Buffalo Bill pulled out his wallet. "Here—buy

yourself a ticket for North Platte. And get on the next train."

That afternoon the fair grounds streamed with people. The stands were crowded before show time.

The performance began with a band of Indians leaping bareback onto ponies and racing around the track. Then the Indians captured a scout, but a troop of army men galloped in and rescued the captive. Cowboys climbed onto blindfolded horses and galloped after Texas steers. With shrill cries they swung their lariats; they roped and tied the animals. Mounted Indians surrounded a plunging herd of buffalo. A Pony Express rider dashed across the field. In front of the grandstand he leaped to the ground, transferred his mail bags to a fresh pony and pounded away. Major North, billed as "The White Chief of the Pawnees," beat the drum for a Pawnee war dance. Across the field, behind six horses, rumbled the old Deadwood Stage. The Indians leaped onto ponies and went whooping after it. With blazing rifles Buffalo Bill and Dr. Carver galloped to the rescue.

It was a ragged performance but full of fire. The audience cheered every dramatic action. At the end they gave Buffalo Bill a storm of applause when he reined his horse before the stand and swept the big hat from his flowing hair. The show was a success.

In his tent, surrounded by newspapermen, Buffalo Bill announced his plan to take the Wild West to New York. When he stepped out of his tent he saw a beaming face.

"Johnny Baker," he said. "I thought you were on your way home."

Johnny's eyes shone. "It was a wonderful show."

The big man smiled. "Yes, it was, Johnny. A real Blowout." He put a hand on the boy's shoulder. "But we're going a long way from Nebraska. You have to go home. Still got that money?"

The boy held up the money. "Take it back, Buffalo Bill. Let me stay with the show."

"What would you do, boy?"

"Anything. I'll hold your horse. I'll shine your boots. I'll carry your guns, your ammunition."

Buffalo Bill looked down. It seemed a long

time before he spoke. "Get my guns out of the tent. We're packing up, Johnny."

They traveled east, making one-day stands in Illinois, Ohio, Pennsylvania. On the Fourth of July, just a year after the Old Glory Blowout, they played in Boston to 25,000 cheering spectators. They moved on to Brooklyn and New York. At Brighton Beach the Wild West was enacted beside the Atlantic Ocean.

At the end of the summer they turned back west. In Chicago the show set up in Humboldt Park, and there a general restlessness broke out. It had been a long season; the Indians were growing homesick and the cowboys independent. Dr. Carver quit the show; he had had enough. Even the animals were restive, pawing the ground and bellowing in their pens. Buffalo Bill paced the show grounds with silent Johnny Baker beside him. A Wild West Show was made up of reckless men and half-wild animals. Could it be held together?

In the grandstand at Humboldt Park was a man named Nate Salsbury. He was a famous dramatic producer, whose "Troubadours" were then playing in a Chicago theater. After the show he called at Buffalo Bill's tent. His enthusiasm was a tonic to Buffalo Bill.

The Wild West Show, he declared, was a great new idea in entertainment, better than any circus. He admired it as a historical exhibition of the American frontier. He thought it had a great future.

That day Buffalo Bill and Nate Salsbury signed a contract. Salsbury became Business Manager of the Wild West Show. He would raise money for its expansion; he would enlarge its organization and direct its tours. On that agreement the two men shook hands.

That night as he looked over the sleeping show grounds, Buffalo Bill hummed his favorite song: "Tenting tonight, tenting tonight, tenting on the old camp ground." The first season was over, and he had a new partner for the bigger seasons ahead.

3
Shipwreck on the River

A high band wagon behind six prancing horses led the parade through the streets of St. Louis. The cowboy band, in ten-gallon hats and buckskin shirts, was a new feature of the show in 1884, and it had a new name—BUFFALO BILL'S WILD WEST. Press agent Burke had added a subtitle: "America's National Entertainment."

Buffalo Bill's new partner, Nate Salsbury, saw the opening performance at the St. Louis Driving

after his return to Nebraska, Major North died.

Buffalo Bill had lost an old friend, a ranching partner and a valuable showman. It would be hard to manage the Indians without Frank North, who knew their language and understood their feelings.

The show moved on, hounded by cold wet weather. Every day cost thousands of dollars, with no money coming in at the ticket windows. Nate Salsbury sent funds to pay the railroad bills, the food and feed bills, the wages of the performers and workmen.

That winter a big exhibition, the Cotton Centennial, was held at New Orleans. Perhaps the Wild West could mend its fortunes there. Instead of disbanding for the winter Buffalo Bill decided to take his show to the crowds at New Orleans.

He and Major Burke went ahead to make arrangements. In charge of the show they left Pony Bob Haslam, an old comrade of Buffalo Bill's from the days of the Pony Express. Haslam was a good horseman but a poor businessman. At Cincinnati he hired a river boat to take the outfit south, with a few performances at river towns along the way.

It was the first time the Wild West had traveled by water—buffalo, steers, mules and horses crowded on the lower deck, Indians, cowboys, musicians and teamsters on the deck above. They were cheerful, heading into warm weather and thinking of big crowds at New Orleans.

Then came the calamity. A few miles below Vicksburg, in the middle of the river and the middle of the night, the showboat collided with a barge. Water poured into the shattered hull. The boat began to sink.

The cowboys swam horses ashore and the Indians climbed onto the undamaged barge. The stagecoach and band wagon stayed afloat. But all the rest was lost. Buffalo, mules, elk and steers were drowned. Rifles, revolvers, ammunition, the loaded wagons, all the show's equipment went to the bottom of the Mississippi. Rainy daybreak showed a soaked and dismal company on the river bank.

To Buffalo Bill in New Orleans came the bad news. It was raining there too, and the show grounds were under water. Buffalo Bill, at the end of his rope, telegraphed his partner: OUTFIT AT BOTTOM OF RIVER. WHAT DO YOU ADVISE?

Nate Salsbury was an indomitable showman who could rise above great obstacles. His answer came: OPEN ON YOUR DATE. HAVE WIRED YOU FUNDS.

Buffalo Bill bought some steers from Texas. He sent to Nebraska for more Indians (half of his Pawnees had quit) and a new herd of buffalo.

The show opened on schedule with twenty-five Indians in the saddle, seven Mexicans, eight cowboys. But the stands were almost empty. The next day rain poured down.

It was a wet winter in New Orleans. The Cotton Exposition was expected to draw a million visitors. But January brought gray skies and an endless sullen rain. The crowds never came.

For forty-four days the Wild West show grounds was a dismal place. Horses stood dripping in their corral; steers and buffalo churned their pens to mud. The cowboys stared gloomily out of their dripping bunk tent. In smoky wigwams the Indians fed their little fires and chanted songs of home.

Another show had come to New Orleans, hoping to draw exposition crowds. In her dressing tent in the Sells Brothers Circus, while the rain came down, sat a trim girlish sharpshooter. She was polishing her rifle barrel while a deep-voiced man talked about Buffalo Bill's show on the muddy Metairie Race Track at the edge of town.

These were Annie Oakley and her husband, Frank Butler. They had traveled with Sells Circus for a year, and they were ready for a change.

One day they visited the Wild West camp. Even in the rain they liked what they saw. At the end of the empty grandstand, near a huddle of tepees, Indians squatted over a cooking fire. A cowboy splashed past in a mudstained slicker. He disappeared into a long tent where, to a wheezy mouth organ, a slow voice was singing:

> *A ten-dollar hoss and a forty-dollar saddle,*
> *And I'm goin' to punchin' Texas cattle.*

Under the grandstand a round-faced boy was practicing target shooting.

Buffalo Bill was not in his tent but Major Burke was there. He told them about the show's bad luck—the death of Major North, the wreck on the river, and now their sharpshooter leaving them. Captain Bogardus couldn't stand the weather, and he wanted to put his four boys in school.

When he learned that Annie Oakley was a shooting star, Arizona John thought they could use her in the Wild West. But not now.

"The green sward our carpet," he quoted grimly, staring out at the field of mud. "Heaven's azure canopy our canvas—" looking up at the leaden sky. Maybe, he concluded, things would be better in the spring.

At that moment the Wild West was $60,000 in debt, and the sky looked as though it would never clear. Anyone less hopeful than Arizona John would have thought the show a failure. Even Buffalo Bill had concluded that fate was against him. He was almost ready to give up.

But Nate Salsbury would soon join them with

his energy and his showmanship. New Indians and cowboys were coming from Nebraska. Soon the show would be rolling again.

They would leave desolate New Orleans for Mobile, Birmingham, Savannah. Then in April they would swing north. This dejected, dripping show was still "America's National Entertainment."

4
Annie Oakley Joins Up

In the warm April sunlight the Louisville baseball grounds looked like a western camp. Across the green infield stood a cluster of wigwams, an empty picket-pole corral, a long mess tent with open sides. In the outfield rose a huge cardboard screen of painted mountains.

A horse cab drove onto the grounds and a man and woman stepped out. The Negro driver unloaded a heavy gun case and a costume trunk.

Then little Annie Oakley and her husband looked around. A man in a white apron came out of the cook tent.

"Where is everybody?" Frank Butler called.

"In the street parade. You're three hours early for the show."

"That's good," said Annie Oakley to her husband. "I need to practice."

He opened the gun trunk, took out a small folding table and laid her guns across it. As he tossed up a glass ball she threw the gun to her shoulder and fired. The target shattered. He threw two balls. Bang! Bang! The glass bubbles vanished. He threw four targets. None of them reached the ground.

From her childhood on an Ohio farm Annie Oakley had been a sharpshooter. With a combination of keen eyesight, timing and coordination she could shoot the head off a running quail or drop a bird on the wing. A trim girlish figure, with a soft voice and a wide warm smile, she was a phenomenal marksman. Frank Butler had been her partner in trick shooting on the stage, but the crowds made her their favorite. So she became the shooting star and he served as her manager.

Across the show grounds came a courtly, courteous man in striped trousers and a long-tailed coat. He took off his derby hat.

"I am Nate Salsbury, Mr. Cody's partner. You are Miss Oakley—Major Burke told me about you. Can you be in costume for today's performance? Can you shoot from horseback? I'll take you to your dressing tent."

An hour later the parade loped into the grounds —whooping Indians in feathered bonnets, Mexicans in bright serapes and huge sombreros, yipping cowboys, light-stepping horses ahead of the battered stagecoach. On the band wagon the cowboy musicians were playing, "Oh! Susanna."

It was not like a circus parade with ponderous draft horses and painted wagons. This outfit was all alive. The cowboys galloped across the field and leaped to the ground. With shrill cries the Indians herded their horses into the corral. When their saddles were pulled off, the pack mules brayed, kicked at each other and rolled on the grass. An old bull buffalo lowered his massive head and pawed the ground. Someone cried, "When do we eat?"

In the cook tent Annie Oakley was introduced to the performers—Frank Richmond, the Master of Ceremonies, Lanky Buck Taylor, the half-breed Bill Bullock, bowlegged Con Groner, and the bearded old Squaw Man who had an Indian wife and two black-eyed children. He was John Nelson but he preferred his Indian name, Cha-sha-sha-na-po-ge-o, which meant "Red Willow Fill the Pipe."

Then Buffalo Bill appeared in a fringed jacket of white buckskin. When he swept off his hat the long hair fell to his shoulders.

"Welcome, Missie. Welcome to the Wild West."

So Annie Oakley joined the show that would be her home for the next seventeen years. And so she was named. To the Indians and cowboys she would always be Missie, their little sister and their friend.

Two hours later the show began. In the grand entry, the whole company paraded round the ring. Then from the empty arena Frank Richmond announced to the crowd:

"Ladies and Gentlemen! The Wild West presents the foremost markswoman in the world, in an exhibition of skill with rifle, shotgun and pistol —the Little Girl of the Western Plains—ANNIE OAKLEY!"

She looked like a girl but she shot like a veteran. On a loping horse she broke targets thrown in the air by a galloping cowboy. She leaped to the ground, ran to her gun stand and shot glass balls thrown by Frank Butler. She aimed a rifle over her shoulder, sighting in a mirror at a silver dish Frank Butler held over his head. As she pulled the trigger the target spun from his hand.

While the crowd roared she caught her pony and raced out of the ring. The rest of the show was full of pounding hoofs, rumbling wheels, war cries and the bang of firearms.

There was always danger that gunfire would scare the horses and frighten women and children in the audience. Now Buffalo Bill saw how to avoid that danger. The show opened with a graceful girl in the huge arena. She began shooting with a pistol; she changed to a rifle, then the louder shotgun. In five minutes she prepared the animals and the audience for the noisy, fast-paced show.

For seventeen years Annie Oakley began the show—the first act after the grand entry. Never in the history of the Wild West did a horse run away or a steer stampede.

Annie Oakley had never been west of the Mississippi but she was billed as the Heroine of the Plains. In her buckskin costume and broad felt hat, with a silver star on its upturned brim, she looked like a western girl. The crowds were fascinated by her charm, vitality and grace as much as by her shooting.

But Johnny Baker was jealous. He wanted to be a star marksman; he was letting his hair grow long like Buffalo Bill. But now a soft-voiced girl was the shooting star. He watched her like a coyote and he kept a coyote's distance.

One morning on the show lot in an Indiana town Johnny Baker was shooting at a paper target under the grandstand. He looked up to see Annie

Oakley there. While she admired the rifle Buffalo
Bill had given him, Johnny scowled at the ground.
He was ready to run away.

But when she asked if he had ever shot a buffalo, the boy's silence melted.

Yes, he had shot a buffalo, a big bull that broke
a leg while they were playing last summer at Pros-
pect Park, New York. But that was not like
shooting on a hunt. Buffalo Bill had promised to
take him hunting in the fall. Buffalo Bill had been
teaching him to shoot, but now he was too busy.

Annie Oakley suggested practicing together.
They might work up some tricks. She would
show him how to aim a rifle over his shoulder.

"Will you?" Johnny cried. "I'll carry your
guns. I'll bring your ammunition from the wagon.
Buffalo Bill told me to watch how you swing
with a target."

Now Johnny Baker had a goddess in his life,
and Annie Oakley had a lasting friend.

In high spirits and fine May weather the show
unloaded in Chicago for a two-week stay. The
parade moved down State Street between cheering crowds.

At the head of the line rode Buffalo Bill on his dappled gray horse, a veteran of the buffalo chase. Then came the band wagon with the cowboys playing "Old Bald Eagle Sail Around." Chief White Eagle and fifteen Pawnee warriors sat bareback on their ponies. Grizzled old "Pack" Smiles led a file of pack mules. Next came a whooping band of Wichitas with Chief Dave in the lead. The Mexican vaqueros rode with jingling spurs and buckskin straps bouncing behind their saddles. In a carriage drawn by matched mustangs sat Annie Oakley and Johnny Baker with rifles across their knees. With a whooping *Ki-yi-yip-a-ou!* cowboys circled a string of long-horned steers. The parade ended with the Deadwood Stage, dented by bullets from bandits in the Black Hills.

Back at the show lot crowds streamed over the grounds, visiting the Indian Village, the buffalo corrals, the pens of bucking horses.

Day after day the crowds came. Money poured into the ticket wagon. This was the success that Buffalo Bill had dreamed of. At midnight he walked over the sleeping grounds. A pony whickered as he passed, an old bull buffalo snorted. His voice hummed, "Tenting tonight, tenting tonight. . . ."

In two years the Wild West Show had survived the disasters of being sunk in the Mississippi, rained out of New Orleans, and $60,000 in debt. Now it was bigger than ever, the safe was bulging with money, the crowds kept coming. "Tenting tonight"—Buffalo Bill was a happy man.

But his restless partner, Nate Salsbury, was planning to make the show still better. They had daring cowboys, red Indians, fine horses. They had the incomparable Annie Oakley. They had famous plainsmen, men who had made history in the western army camps and on the cattle trails. But they had no famous Indian. They had no members of the most famous of western tribes—the Sioux.

Ever since Custer's massacre by Sitting Bull's warriors in 1876, the nation's attention had been focused on the defiant Sioux and their proud chief. Since the defeat of Custer the Sioux had been humbled by the United States Army and confined to reservation lands. Sitting Bull had fled to Canada. When he came back to Dakota Territory he was taken prisoner. Now he was on the reservation at Standing Rock, brooding on the downfall of his people.

Buffalo Bill and Sitting Bull had been enemies during the Indian wars. But now they could be friends.

Before the show left Chicago, Nate Salsbury had a bold and exciting idea. He would hire the most famous chief of the most famous Indian nation. Then the Wild West would have three stars —Buffalo Bill, Annie Oakley and Sitting Bull.

5
The Chief
at Standing Rock

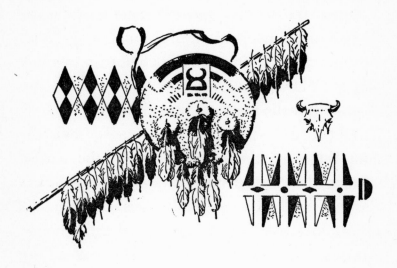

Far up the Missouri River a great rock rises above the gaunt plains of South Dakota. Standing Rock, the Sioux called it. It was the landmark of their reservation.

Early in June, 1885, a big man in a buckskin jacket and a ten-gallon hat strode into the office of the Indian Agent at Fort Yates near Standing Rock. He introduced himself as Major John M. Burke, publicity director for Buffalo Bill's Wild

West. He had come to see Sitting Bull, to offer him a contract to tour the eastern cities with Buffalo Bill's road show.

Sitting Bull's camp was on Grand River at the far end of the reservation, fifty miles away. With two interpreters Major Burke climbed into a box wagon. They swung southwest, over the ocean of grass and the blowing June flowers.

All that day and the next they rocked over the long ridges of the reservation. On the second evening they pulled up at a scattering of lodges above Grand River. Smoke seeped from the supper fires and dogs sniffed at old cattle bones. Arizona John got down stiffly. He took off his Stetson, removed three hairpins from his knotted hair, and raised a hand in greeting. He was at the camp of the most famous Indian in America, the villain of Custer's Massacre, Chief Sitting Bull.

Tatanka Iyotake was the chief's Sioux name. It meant, "He came into our midst, strong as a buffalo bull, and sat down."

Sitting Bull was a combination of strength and deliberation. He had a massive head and bull-broad shoulders, a tapering waist and neat small feet. Twin braids of hair, tied with strips of otter-skin, swung at his waist. His stern face was pitted with smallpox scars from an epidemic in his youth. He had killed his first buffalo at ten, his first enemy at fourteen. He had risen to leadership of the Hunkpapa tribe, the fiercest clan in the Sioux nation. His warriors had ambushed Custer's Cavalry on the Little Big Horn in Montana. Since then he had endured exile, starvation and imprisonment. Now he lived with his two wives and ten children in a remote camp on the Standing Rock reservation.

He came out of his tepee and faced his visitor. They were two big men, Burke and Bull, and both were fond of ceremony.

Arizona John, his hand still raised, spoke of his pride at meeting a chief whose fame was known afar.

While the interpreter repeated that in Sioux, the chief stood impassive. Finally he spoke. In a deep, deliberate voice he welcomed his visitor with flowing hair. But why had he come to see a chief now tethered like a horse on the agency lands?

Major Burke made his proposal. He wanted Sitting Bull and a party of warriors and their women to travel with the Wild West Show. They would be well paid, well fed, well treated. They would have fresh beef in their tepees and fine horses to ride. They would see the white man's towns and cities. At the end of the summer they would be brought back on the railroad to Standing Rock.

After that long speech Sitting Bull did not answer. He led the way to his wigwam, limping from a wound received in a battle in his youth. While the long June twilight softened the prairie, they ate their supper and lit their pipes. And still *Tatanka Iyotake* did not give his answer.

Sitting Bull had already seen something of the white man's world. A year before, he had been taken on a tour of the eastern states where he was exhibited to curious crowds. He had been promised an interview with the President, in Washington, but the promise was broken. Now he had no reason to trust the white men nor to want to travel with them.

But the next morning he had decided; he would

join Buffalo Bill's show. So the wagon rattled back to the Missouri, with Major Burke jostling happily among Sitting Bull and eight of his tribesmen.

At the Agency House he wrote out a contract:

This agreement entered into this sixth day of June, 1885. . . . I, John M. Burke, do hereby agree to pay Sitting Bull Fifty (50.00) Dollars per week, to be paid weekly every Saturday night; Five (5) Indians at twenty-five (25.00) Dollars; three Indian women at Fifteen (15.00) Dollars per month, to be paid monthly; and William Halsey, interpreter, to be paid Sixty (60.00) Dollars per month. . . . Sitting Bull and party do hereby agree to travel with the Buffalo Bill Wild West Show . . . for summer season of four months. . . . John M. Burke does also agree to pay all expenses . . . of the party from the Show to Standing Rock at expiration of this contract.

Sitting Bull listened carefully while the interpreter translated this agreement into Sioux. Then he spoke to the interpreter and the interpreter turned to Major Burke.

"He wants the right to sell his photographs."
Arizona John added a line to the contract:

P.S. Sitting Bull is to have sole right to sell his own Photographs and Autographs.

When the others had signed, the scowling chief drew his picture of a crouching buffalo and misspelled his name: "Sietting Bull."

Meanwhile the Wild West Show had traveled east from Chicago. On June 12th, while they were making camp at Buffalo, New York, two cabs pulled up in the arena. Out stepped Arizona John, beaming with pride and pleasure. Behind him came Sitting Bull and his party.

The Indians had been bewildered by their long train trip from Dakota, but here, on the Wild West show grounds, they were at home. They saw smoke curling up from cooking fires beside the Pawnee lodges. They smelled the dust of steers and horses; they heard the snort of buffalo and the crack of rifle fire from the target range.

Then Buffalo Bill appeared. *Pahaska*—Long Hair—the Sioux called him. He raised a hand and spoke to Sitting Bull. The chief raised a hand in

friendship, palm outward. They knew each other
from past meetings on the plains.

Now Major Burke had a new subject for publicity. He wrote newspaper stories about Sitting
Bull and brought reporters to see the storied
chief. He had Buffalo Bill and Sitting Bull pose
together for photographers. In this picture Buffalo Bill wore his most handsome hunting shirt
and Sitting Bull wore a war bonnet of two hundred eagle feathers.

During the season thousands of those photo-
graphs were sold on the show grounds. Major
Burke did not need to identify the two famous
Americans. He entitled the picture "Foes in '76,
Friends in '85."

6
Sitting Bull Adopts
a Daughter

Sitting Bull was given a tepee of his own with his name lettered over the opening, and a buffalo robe to sit on. When the gates were opened crowds streamed through the Indian village to stare at the War Chief of the Fighting Sioux. They saw the scars on his chest and forearms; the show program explained that before Custer's battle the chief had offered a hundred pieces of flesh to the Great Spirit and then had danced the Sun Dance, hour after hour, until he had a vision of victory for his people.

In the grand entry, when all the performers rode around the arena, Major Burke sat with Sitting Bull in an open buggy. Under his war bonnet the chief's dark eyes moved scornfully over the packed grandstand.

The crowd might have cheered the famous chief, but they didn't. The scornful pride in his face reminded them of tales of Indian cruelty. Sitting Bull, one stubborn legend said, had shot General Custer and slashed off his long hair. Instead of cheering, the crowd jeered at the murderer of Custer.

At the end of the arena Sitting Bull jumped down from the buggy. His defiant eyes swept the grandstand. Then he lurched away, limping from that old wound of his youth. At that moment Major Burke thought his star attraction was ready to go back to Standing Rock.

In the arena a voice was announcing, ". . . in feats of skill with pistol, rifle and shotgun, the Girl of the Western Plains!"

The grim chief turned around. He watched

while graceful Annie Oakley shot glass balls out
of the air. A cowboy galloped in, swinging targets
on a leather thong. Annie Oakley leaned from a
buckskin pony and snatched a pistol from the
grass. She smashed the whirling targets—one, two,
three.

Above the roar of the crowd boomed the voice
of Sitting Bull.

"Ho! Ho! Was-te! Wa-kan!"

When Annie Oakley ran out of the ring, the
chief shambled after her. Major Burke found
him at the door of her tent. His somber face had
broken into a smile like sunrise. "Wan-tan-yeya,
Ci-sci-la," he said, meaning "Little Straight
Shooter, Little Sure Shot."

As the days passed, Sitting Bull proved to be
a combination of impassive man and curious boy.
He discovered popcorn candy at the refreshment
stand and bought ten boxes at a time. While curious
visitors pressed around his tepee, he sat on his buffalo robe smoking his long-stemmed pipe and
munching the candy.

When the show moved from Buffalo to Pitts-
burgh he watched the tent crew driving iron

stakes. They stood in a circle, each man with a sledge hammer. As they swung in sequence, one after another, the heavy stake sank into the ground.

The burly chief took a sledge from the wagon. With a grunt of pleasure he edged into that circle of sweating roustabouts. The most famous personage in the Wild West, with a string of bear claws around his neck and two eagle feathers in his hair, never grew tired of driving tent stakes.

Early one morning when they were setting up on a new lot, a stranger wandered through the grounds. "Where is Sitting Bull?" he asked. "He killed my brother at Custer's Massacre. Where is he?"

Then he saw the circle of swinging, sweating tent men.

"There he is, the murderer!" cried the stranger. He pulled out a revolver.

Sitting Bull had not lost the wary senses of the war trail and the hunt. He crouched in the circle and swung his heavy hammer. It flew backward, over his shoulder; it dropped the gunman to the ground.

A couple of cowboys laid him on a bale of hay. Sitting Bull recovered his sledge and went on driving tent stakes.

Half an hour later the stranger, rubbing a lump on his head, walked out of the show grounds.

Sitting Bull, like all Indians, was fond of children, and he was a hero to them. Clusters of small boys hung around his tent and followed him across the lot. They copied his limping gait and stuck paper in their hair for want of eagle feathers. At the refreshment stand he bought them popcorn and candy.

Newsboys and shoeshine boys roamed over the grounds, looking for business. Sitting Bull was their best customer. He couldn't read a paper and his moccasins wouldn't take a shine, but he handed out nickels and dimes all day long. His Saturday night pay was gone before the week was over.

Sitting Bull could not understand how in the white man's world some people could be rich and others poor. And he was amazed at the size of the white man's cities.

"The white people are so many," he told a newspaper reporter, "that if every Indian in the West killed one with every step he took, the dead would not be missed among you."

When reporters asked him about Custer's defeat, the chief said: "Nobody knows who killed Custer; every Indian fired at him. Custer was a brave warrior, but he made a mistake. The Indians honored him and did not scalp him. I fought for my people. My people said I was right. I will answer to my people. I will answer for the dead of my people. Let the palefaces do the same on their side."

Life on the Wild West lot was friendly. The Indians and cowboys acted out warfare in the arena; then they ate watermelons together and smoked in the shade of the show wagons.

In the mellow atmosphere Buffalo Bill made generous statements about the Indians. "I never shot an Indian but what I regretted it afterwards," he told reporters. "In nine cases out of ten when there is trouble between white men and Indians, it will be found that the white man is responsible for the dispute by breaking faith with them."

Once Major Burke gave an Indian a cigar, and

promised him "heap big cigars" later. Buffalo Bill did not let his press agent forget that promise. "Don't ever break a promise to an Indian," he said. "Get a box of cigars in town and charge it to me. Don't forget."

To the newspapermen Buffalo Bill said, "Indians expect a man to keep his word. They don't understand how a man can lie. Most of them would as soon cut off a leg as tell a lie."

About Custer's battle Buffalo Bill said, "The defeat of Custer was not a massacre. The Indians were being pursued by skilled fighters with orders to kill. They had their wives and little ones to protect, and they were fighting for their existence."

Sitting Bull respected his old adversary. Through his translator he told reporters that *Pahaska*—Long Hair—was a great scout. He was also a sincere and honest man.

Traveling, working, living together, the show company was like a big, bustling family. Buffalo Bill had virtually adopted Johnny Baker; he called him "son" and gave him advice on everything from money to target shooting. The plainsman's only son, Kit Carson Cody, had died in infancy.

Johnny Baker filled an empty place in Buffalo Bill's life.

It was common for an Indian Chief to adopt people into his tribe, or even into his family. In years past Sitting Bull had adopted three brothers. One was a frightened Assiniboin boy left orphaned after a battle with the Sioux. He ran to Sitting Bull, crying "Big Brother!" Young Siting Bull had no brother of his own, but in that cry he found one. In the warmth of his tepee he fed the boy, dressed him in deerskins and painted his face. Outside he gave away a horse in his honor. Ten years later he adopted a French missionary, Jean Baptiste Marie Genin, who had become a friend of the Sioux; and still later he adopted a third brother, a white messenger captured by the Sioux while he crossed their hunting grounds above the Yellowstone.

Now in his tent on the show grounds the great chief went through a solemn ceremony and adopted Annie Oakley as his daughter. So she became a Sioux princess. Though they could not speak each other's language, the tiny markswoman and the massive chief understood each other's feelings. Little Sure Shot, he named her. He gave her presents: a feathered headdress, a quiver of his finest arrows, and a pair of beaded moccasins that had been made for him by an Indian daughter who had died.

7

"We're on the Way"

Show life was the clicking of the rails at midnight and the dark country flowing by. It was the unloading at daybreak, the wagons creaking to the exhibition grounds, the smell of coffee and bacon from the cook tent. It was the long street parade, band playing, horses prancing, people lining the sidewalks while the cowboys clattered past. It was the roar of ten thousand voices in the arena, and the night silence when the stars looked down on the tents of the Indians—like a Pawnee camp far out on the Laramie Plains. It was loading up and moving on.

One-night stands were strenuous. The show people were glad when they could shake out and settle down for an unbroken week or two.

In Boston the Old South Meeting House on Washington Street had watched two hundred years of history. It had seen Puritans in long black coats and steeple hats walking to church in the winter snow. It had seen marching British redcoats and defiant Sons of Liberty. It had seen men dressed in paint and feathers hurrying to the harbor where three British vessels were preparing to unload tea.

Through narrow streets on a summer day in 1885 came the Wild West parade. On his old hunting horse, Charley, rode Buffalo Bill, doffing his big hat to solid walls of people. Bareback on a spotted pony came Sitting Bull in a war bonnet of eagle feathers. From files of Indians, war whoops quavered in the winding street. Annie Oakley, in fringed buckskin, with the silver star on her upturned hat, waved from an open buggy. Then came scouts, Mexican vaqueros, Nebraska cowboys. With a creak of leather and a scuffle of hoofs the newest part of America passed through historic Boston.

On foot, on bicycles, in carts and carriages crowds followed to the show grounds in Beacon Park. They swarmed over the lot, past the Indian village and the stockade of wild horses. They looked into a tent where Johnny Baker was polishing Annie Oakley's pistols. They crowded around a tepee where Sitting Bull was scrawling his name on a stack of photographs.

Everywhere the show went, Sitting Bull was a center of interest. But in Boston he got more attention than even Buffalo Bill—or "Bison William," as the Boston papers called him. To please the crowds the chief was kept in public view. Following his appearance in the arena he climbed onto the bandstand and tapped his feet to the music.

After the show he received reporters in his tepee, greeting them with a solemn "How!" and presenting his photograph. One newspaper writer found a resemblance between Sitting Bull and

New England's greatest statesman. He wrote: "They are the faces of thoughtful men, these Indian chieftains. Their leader, Sitting Bull, has especially strong lines in his countenance which is something of a reminder of the features of Daniel Webster."

Major Burke, never missing a chance for new publicity, invited the press to a Wild West barbecue. Over a pit of glowing embers a Texas steer was broiled and basted. The meal was followed by a ceremony in Sitting Bull's tepee.

Nate Salsbury, Buffalo Bill, Major Burke and a dozen reporters bared their heads and sat cross-legged in a circle. Sitting Bull lit a long-stemmed pipe, fringed with eagle feathers, and puffed out three clouds of smoke. He passed the pipe around the circle, and each man puffed in turn. When the pipe came back to Sitting Bull he blew smoke to the four winds. Then in deliberate Sioux phrases he named Nate Salsbury *Wah-see-sha-e-ton-sha* —Little White Chief—and adopted him into the Sioux nation.

Nate Salsbury pledged lifelong friendship to

the Sioux, and Sitting Bull said that if he were at home on Grand River he would give Little White Chief a pony. Now he knocked out the ashes from the pipe and gave it to Salsbury as a souvenir of the ceremony. After a general handshake they all went out for more barbecued beef.

In Boston the Wild West held its first night performance. Electric light was in an early stage of development; a few seasons later the show would have its own electrical plant and complete illumination. But here at Boston new calcium flares mounted on poles flooded the arena. In that white light against the surrounding darkness the performance was more dramatic than ever.

Light was all-important to the sharpshooters. When the calcium flares were first mounted, Frank Butler worried about that unnatural illumination. Before the stands were open he took Annie Oakley and Johnny Baker to the empty arena. Johnny threw glass balls in all directions. Bang! Bang! Bang! Annie Oakley shattered them with her rifle. When they had repeated it three times, in different angles under the lights, Frank Butler was satisfied.

"Missie," he said, taking Annie's gun, "I guess you could hit them in the dark."

From Boston the show moved north through New Hampshire and Vermont and into Canada. In Montreal thousands followed the street parade to the show grounds on the St. Lawrence River. The first afternoon the sky darkened and the show went on in a summer downpour. Annie Oakley shot targets through a curtain of rain and the horses splashed through standing water. Under a roofed grandstand the crowd cheered wildly. Then the sky brightened. While Indians ambushed the wagon train the sun streamed down and the wet ponies shone like paint.

All through eastern Canada the newspapers ran columns on Sitting Bull. After Custer's defeat, the Sioux chief had fled to Canada. The Canadians were glad to remember that Sitting Bull had found refuge across their border when General Terry's "walk-a-heaps" and his "pony soldiers" pursued him.

The newspapers revived many legends of Sitting Bull. One story said that he was really a

Canadian half-breed, born near old Fort Garry on the Winnipeg prairies. Another said he was a devout Catholic, converted by the famous missionary Father de Smet. (It is true that Sitting Bull had once protected the priest in a Sioux camp, and at that time Father de Smet gave him a silver crucifix. Often the chief wore the crucifix along with a necklace of bear claws. He liked all kinds of jewelry.) Another writer declared that Sitting Bull was an admirer of Napoleon and had carefully studied his military campaigns. After the Battle of the Little Big Horn, it was said, Sitting Bull saw the ghost of Custer. The ghost told him he would die of treachery in fifteen years. That gave Sitting Bull five more years to live; it would prove an accurate prophecy.

The show was a great success in Canada, and Nate Salsbury was confident it would be an equal success in England. That was his greatest dream. At midnight on the show train after a triumphant week in Toronto, he turned to Buffalo Bill.

"We're on the way," he declared, "and we won't stop till we have reached the heights. Cody,

I'll land you at the foot of the throne of England."

By the end of September they were back in the United States, playing at Columbus, Ohio. Some army officers stationed at Columbus barracks came to the show. As they approached his tepee, Sitting Bull's dark eyes sharpened. He jumped to his feet. "How! How!" His pockmarked face broke into a smile as he shook hands with Lieutenant McMartin.

"This young man," said Sitting Bull through his interpreter, "rolled cigarettes for me at Fort Randall."

The officer nodded. Then he rolled a cigarette, touched it with a match and handed it over. While the chief smoked it down, Lieutenant McMartin explained to reporters that he had once been in charge of the army's top prisoner at Fort Randall on the upper Missouri.

The season ended at St. Louis in a cold October rain. To advertise the show Major Burke took Sitting Bull downtown. The chief was dressed in his war bonnet and silver arm bands.

Across a crowded hotel lobby the chief's dark eyes singled out a rugged, bearded man with gold braid on his shoulders. *Hiah!* he muttered—the old alert of the Plains Indians.

It was Three Stars, his old pursuer in the Bad Lands, the most famous Indian fighter in the West.

General Carr shouldered through the crowd and the two stood face to face. Three Stars greeted him like an old comrade, but Sitting Bull stood silent. He wanted to get away from the crowds of white men. He was ready to go home to the empty plains.

On October 11th they had an early supper in the cook tent, with the band playing "Auld Lang Syne" to mark the season's end. The animals would be wintered in St. Louis, but the company would scatter. Next year there would be a bigger show, a longer train, better equipment. Nate Salsbury and Buffalo Bill wished them all a good winter and a happy reunion in the spring.

While the band played "Home, Sweet Home," they said their good-byes. Then they scattered in all directions—Buffalo Bill and Johnny Baker to Nebraska, Major Burke to Washington, Nate Salsbury to New York, Annie Oakley and her husband to her childhood home in the woods of

Darke County, Ohio. The cowboys went to western towns and ranches, the Mexicans to adobe houses in the sun. Sitting Bull led his little band of Sioux back to the wind-swept plains beyond Standing Rock.

8
Annie Oakley's Battle

A million people had seen the Wild West in
1885 and the show had made a fortune. That fall
Buffalo Bill enlarged his ranch at North Platte. He
built a sixteen-room mansion and a long barn with
SCOUT'S REST RANCH lettered on its roof.
Three thousand cattle and a thousand horses
ranged over his huge pastures.

The rest of the Wild West profits went back
into the show, making it larger and better for the

new season. When the performers gathered in St. Louis in the spring, they found a new show train on the tracks—a long train of white and gold cars lettered BUFFALO BILL'S WILD WEST. There were new cowboys, new cowgirls, a larger Indian camp.

In place of Sitting Bull the program advertised two Sioux chiefs, American Horse and Rocky Bear. Featured new cowboys were Jolting Jim Kidd from Nebraska, Dick Bean of Texas, Big Dick Johnson from Wyoming, and Sunday Jim Mitchell, the Cowboy Preacher of the Plains. Johnny Baker was there, an inch taller now, striding in the shadow of Buffalo Bill, and glad to be back on the show grounds after a winter in school. Annie Oakley appeared in a new shooting costume. Expert with a needle as with a gun, she had made a new wardrobe during the long winter evenings in the Ohio farmhouse.

For a week they played to crowded stands in St. Louis. Then on a moonlit night in May the engine whistled, a brakeman swung a lantern down the track and the long show train pulled away.

They played two days in Terre Haute, Indi-

ana, two days in Dayton, Ohio (where Annie
Oakley's sisters came to watch her), two days in
Wheeling, West Virginia. There Buffalo Bill had
his only accident in thirty years in the arena. While
enacting a duel with an Indian warrior, the great
scout caught his foot in the Indian pony's bridle.
Keeping his mount, he wrenched his foot free.
But after the performance his ankle swelled like a
saddlebag.

"First time I was ever downed by an Indian,"
said Buffalo Bill.

On Memorial Day the show unloaded in Washington. This season the cowboy musicians rode on
white horses instead of in a band wagon. In new
red shirts and ten-gallon hats, playing "Marching
Through Georgia," they led the parade past the
White House. The Indians loosed a chorus of
war cries toward the lodge of the Great White
Father and Sergeant Bates, the flag-bearer, dipped
his colors.

During the parade the sky darkened. At noon,
with a roll of thunder, the downpour came. Buffalo Bill, still limping from his twisted ankle, stared
gloomily at the drowned grounds. He wanted a

success in Washington; it seemed a kind of symbol
—the national entertainment in the national cap-
ital.

In streaming slickers the cowboys got their
horses saddled. As one of the girl riders was mount-
ing, a crack of lightning came. The startled pony
threw her against a fence. Two cowboys carried
her off, rain pelting her white still face.

Buffalo Bill pulled at his pointed beard and
trudged through the mud. It looked like a bad be-
ginning.

Then, as suddenly as it had started, the rain
stopped. The clouds opened. Out of a washed
blue sky the sun streamed down. A special train
arrived and a thousand people poured out of the
cars. Down the track another train was whistling.

Buffalo Bill came smiling to the headquarters
tent with Johnny Baker splashing at his side. While
Johnny wiped off his hero's boots, the plainsman
hummed: "Tenting on the old camp ground."

After a triumphant week in Washington they
moved on to Philadelphia. In two weeks the show
played to two hundred thousand cheering spectators.

High spirits ruled the lot—except in the tent with its neat placard ANNIE OAKLEY. There, in pain and darkness, a courageous showgirl was fighting a silent battle.

During the last show in Washington, in the midst of her act Annie Oakley had felt a stabbing pain in her ear. She broke her last target and ran off to a storm of applause. In her tent the doctor examined her ear, finding a tiny insect sting. He left her with a dressing of cotton and sweet oil, and a throbbing, deepening pain.

For two weeks the pain continued. At show time she pulled her broad hat over the swollen ear and ran into the arena. With a tense concentration she steadied her hands and did her shooting. At the gate Frank Butler was waiting. He helped her back to the tent. While she lay on her cot he bathed the inflamed ear with warm water and begged her to go to the hospital. She shook her head grimly—she couldn't miss a show.

From Philadelphia the Wild West moved to Staten Island, across the harbor from New York, for an all-summer stay. At daylight on June 26th they unloaded. A few hours later they were ready for the great New York street parade—the draft horses brushed and curried, Indians in fresh paint and feathers, Mexicans wearing their brightest serapes, cowboys combing out their mustangs' manes.

But in Annie Oakley's tent the doctor looked at a clinical thermometer and shook his head. She had a high temperature. She must lie in bed until the fever passed.

At the landing a ferryboat waited to take the parade across the harbor. From her tent Annie Oakley heard shouts and cries and the clatter of hoofs. Over her open wardrobe trunk a new costume was laid out—fringed skirt and jacket, soft hat with a silver star on its upturned brim, the embroidered saddle cloth with her name in gold. Across the grounds the band began to play.

Her head swaying and swimming, Annie Oakley got out of bed and began to dress. As she buttoned her jacket a wrangler came from the corral, twirling a halter rope.

"Saddle my horse!" she cried.

She reached the ferryboat as the Deadwood

Stage lumbered aboard. She slipped down from the saddle and looked up at anxious Frank Butler and beaming Major Burke. Her radiant smile assured them. She was ready for the great New York parade.

It was the only parade of the summer and the longest they would ever make. The ferry landed at Twenty-third Street; they clattered over the runway and formed in line. The band struck up, horses stamped and whinnied, Nate Salsbury shrilled a whistle and they moved away. It was a long parade route—past miles of brownstone house fronts, past the splendid doorways of Fifth Avenue, past the crowded walks and windows of Broadway.

Sitting sidesaddle, shoulders straight, head thrown back and smiling, Annie Oakley waved to thousands and tried to forget the throbbing in her head. "Cowboys rode like conquerors," stated the New York *Herald*, "between the mansions and hotels of Fifth Avenue." But Annie Oakley rode in pain.

After three hours in the blazing sun the parade

ended. While a crowd watched from the Battery, they boarded a boat for Staten Island. As she slid down from her horse, Annie Oakley fainted.

For three days and nights she tossed in her darkened tent on the show grounds. "Blood poisoning," the doctor said. Frank Butler sat at the bedside, bathing her fevered face. On the fourth day the fever broke and she slept like a child.

The next afternoon, with her hat hiding the white bandage, Annie Oakley dashed into the arena. In six quick shots she put out six candles on a turning wheel. For seventeen years she would not miss another performance.

Buffalo Bill Cody astride his white stallion Isham. With his wide hat, pointed beard and long hair falling to his shoulders, he was a familiar figure to thousands of cheering spectators.

"Defending the Wagon Train" was one of the most popular spectacles put on by the Wild West Show. This drama, with its gunsmoke and its rattle of pistol fire, looked so real that the audiences leaped from their seats and whooped like Indians.

John C. Hemmert, New York

Buffalo Bill holds the reins, and beside him sits Nate Salsbury, the famous dramatic producer who was Cody's partner and business manager for many years.

Sitting Bull, the Sioux chief whose warriors had ambushed Custer's cavalry on the Little Big Horn in 1876, joined the Wild West Show nine years later.

Another performer joined the show in 1885. She was Annie Oakley, the tiny sharpshooter who electrified audiences here and abroad with her marksmanship.

Johnny Baker, who had been with the Wild West Show since boyhood, throws glass balls into the air while Buffalo Bill shoots them.

opposite: *This poster shows just a few of the many places where Buffalo Bill's Wild West Show was given a rousing welcome: London, France, Germany and Rome above; and the Chicago World's Fair of 1893 below.*

RECEIVED BY POPE LEO XIII, VATICAN ROME

PRESIDENT CARNOT FRANCE

H.I.M QUEEN VICTORIA WINDSOR CASTLE

NEW YORK DAY

WHERE WE WERE

"*Little Sure Shot*" *was a phenomenal markswoman, as this poster shows. Whether she was on horseback, on a bicycle or on the ground—even sighting in a mirror and shooting over her shoulder—her aim was always true.*

left: "*Foes in '76, Friends in '85*" *was the caption under the photograph of Sitting Bull and Buffalo Bill. Thousands of these pictures were sold on the Wild West show grounds.*

Brown Brothers

The buffalo hunt was another favorite act. Crowds were thrilled as mounted cowboys and Indians, rifles blazing, attacked the plunging herd.

*Visitors to the Indian Village could see chiefs straight from
frontier history. Here are some of them, with their squaws and
children, against a painted background of mountains.*

"Ladies and gentlemen," boomed the announcer, "Buffalo Bill and Nate Salsbury proudly present America's national entertainment, the one and only, genuine and authentic, unique and original Wild West Show!"

9

The Camp on Staten Island

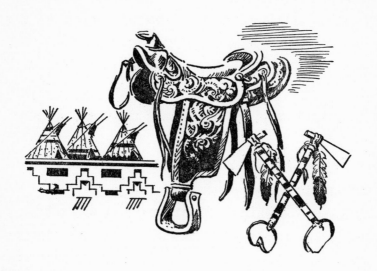

That summer of 1886 thousands of New Yorkers took the ferry to Staten Island. They steamed
past the immigrant station at Castle Garden and
rounded Bedloe's Island where a massive pedestal
was ready to support the Goddess of Liberty;
later that year the great statue would arrive from
France and be erected in New York harbor. They
landed at the Wild West show grounds.

For those visitors a thirty-minute boat ride took

them to the western frontier. Beyond corrals of buffalo and elk, horses and cattle, the Black Hills of Dakota loomed up on a huge scenic background. Under the rugged hills spread the tepees of the Indian village. Mexican vaqueros sprawled in the shade of covered wagons. Cowboys sat on the top rail of the horse corral. From the target range came the crack of rifles and the tang of gunpowder.

In the Indian village squaw man John Nelson sat talking Sioux with his Oglalla wife and two dark-eyed children. Sioux and Pawnee warriors swung in fringed hammocks in the oak grove—they had bought the hammocks with their first month's pay. Over the grounds strolled Indian women draped in striped blankets and checked tablecloths. Indian children clung like monkeys to rope swings under the maple trees.

People came to Staten Island again and again, until they knew the Indians and the cowboys by name and the bucking horses by reputation. They peered into the tents—at Annie Oakley's gun trunk and at the shriveled scalp of Yellow Hand tacked to Buffalo Bill's ridgepole.

They nodded to Chief American Horse and his small son, who had been named "American Colt" by New York newspapermen. That stolid little savage said "How," shook hands gravely, and was reported "ready to wrestle any white boy up to the age of four."

The visitors looked through the fence rails at the outlaw horses—"Suicide," "Lightning" and "Dynamite." They asked broncobuster Tom Clayton how to ride a wild horse. His answer was direct and simple. "Doggone it, jest sit in the saddle and don't get skeart."

When the stands began to fill for the afternoon performance the camp came to life. Cowboys roped and saddled their horses. The Indians daubed themselves with paint and put on their feathered bonnets. Teamsters hitched mules to the Deadwood Stage and oxen to the covered wagons.

Frank Richmond, in big hat and buckskin costume, strode across the arena and mounted a rocklike pedestal under the mimic mountains. He was the "orator" or announcer of the show. His deep voice carried over the whole horseshoe-shaped grandstand:

LADIES AND GENTLEMEN: BUFFALO BILL
AND NATE SALSBURY PROUDLY PRESENT
AMERICA'S NATIONAL ENTERTAINMENT,
THE ONE AND ONLY, GENUINE AND AU-
THENTIC, UNIQUE AND ORIGINAL WILD
WEST SHOW.

Onto the oval track came the grand review,
with twenty thousand voices cheering.

Many famous visitors saw the show that season.
Thomas A. Edison complimented Annie Oakley
on her shooting and signed his name in her autograph book. Buffalo Bill showed the great inventor
through the Indian village and entertained him
at supper in the cook tent. Edison stayed for a
second performance, at night, under new electric
arc lights, his own invention. That summer Thomas A. Edison began a lasting friendship with Buffalo Bill.

The Governor of New York, David Bennett
Hill, came to the show with New York City's
Mayor William Russell Grace. Governor Hill was
a bachelor, a habitually grave and silent man. But
when the Deadwood Stage was ambushed and

the guns were firing, he stood up in his box and whooped like an Indian.

P. T. Barnum, America's most famous circus man, walked through the grounds and sat through two performances in the arena. Though it was a rival show, he praised the Wild West as a magnificent spectacle. "When Nate Salsbury takes this show to Europe," he said, "it will astonish the Old World."

Another distinguished and enthusiastic visitor was Mark Twain. In his young manhood the great humorist had crossed the plains in a stagecoach and had lived in the mining camps of Nevada. He recognized the historical accuracy of the Wild West as well as its dramatic appeal.

After his second visit he wrote Buffalo Bill a letter.

Dear Mr. Cody:

I have now seen your Wild West show two days in succession. It brought back vividly the breezy wild life of the plains and the Rocky Mountains. Down to its smallest detail the show is genuine—cowboys, vaqueros, Indians, stagecoach, costumes and all; it is wholly free from sham and insincerity and the effects it produced upon me were identical with those wrought upon me a long time ago by the same spectacles on the frontier. . . . It is often said on the other side of the water that none of the exhibitions which we send to England are purely and distinctively American. If you will take the Wild West Show over there, you can remove the reproach.

Yours truly,
Mark Twain

There was no performance on Sunday but the ferryboats were crowded and people streamed through the grounds all day. The Wild West camp itself was a western spectacle.

Each Sunday morning Sunday Jim Mitchell, the Cowboy Preacher, rounded up a congregation and held a church service under the cardboard mountains. Once his sermon was interrupted when some restless buffalo broke out of their corral. Sunday Jim leaped onto a pony and drove them back. He finished his sermon in the saddle.

One Sunday afternoon Annie Oakley took a carriage drive with her husband. When she saw a swarm of children behind the iron fence of an orphanage, she stopped and left a message.

Next day in the arena she raced her pony to the end of the stand and waved to fifty special guests. For a moment the orphans' shrill voices drowned the cowboy band.

That was good publicity, as well as a kindness. Major Burke quickly sent free tickets to all the orphanages in New York. "Annie Oakley Day" found the stands filled with excited children. They went home with their stomachs full and their eyes shining.

One day in September a reporter brought a friend to the show, introducing him to everyone in sight. He was Steele McKaye, famous dramatist and theatrical producer. McKaye admired the skill, daring and drama of the performance. After the show he told Nate Salsbury there was nothing like it in the world.

When Salsbury spoke of the approaching end of the season, McKaye asked a question. Why not present the show under roof, in a vast indoor arena where they could play all winter?

Then they were called to a barbecue supper.

But an idea had started in Nate Salsbury's mind. Throughout the meal he kept asking about indoor staging, lighting, seating capacity, quarters for men and animals.

A month later Cody and Salsbury engaged Steele McKaye to stage the Wild West Show at Madison Square Garden for the winter season.

10
War Cries
in Madison Square

The present Madison Square Garden is a huge coliseum, bigger than a circus tent, a mile away from Madison Square. But it keeps the name of New York's first huge indoor arena.

The original Madison Square Garden was in the heart of old New York, on Twenty-sixth Street and Madison Avenue. It contained a spacious stage and a big open arena framed by a U-shaped gallery.

In the fall of 1886, while the Wild West toured west to Chicago and the Mississippi River, a clatter of hammers filled the old Madison Square Garden. On the huge floor carpenters assembled a frontier scene, with a sweep of sagebrush plain breaking into colored buttes and mountains. Perched on lofty ladders, painters sketched a mountain panorama, and workmen set up light towers. Teamsters unloaded bales of canvas, tons of paint, huge coils of rope and wire. Through the din and clatter strode disheveled Steele McKaye.

In November Buffalo Bill arrived with his Indians and cowboys, his stagecoach and covered wagons, his buffalo, steers, and broncos. McKaye then turned director, drilling the Indians and cowboys in a series of dramatic episodes. For its indoor show the Wild West would have a pageant-like sequence of action.

Opening night, on the evening before Thanksgiving, was a festive occasion. In flag-draped boxes sat General Sherman, General Sheridan, the Reverend Henry Ward Beecher, Governor Hill of New York and the widow of General Custer.

Nine thousand people crowded the huge galleries to the roof.

The overhead beams were draped with bunting. The floor was covered with fresh tanbark. Flood-lights played on the scenic background. From the cowboy band on a side stage came "The Star-Spangled Banner."

As the music faded the lights went dim. A ghostly clatter of hoofs filled the vast hall and from the looming mountains came the voice of Buffalo Bill.

LADIES AND GENTLEMEN: THE WILD WEST PRESENTS THE UNIQUE AND UN-PARALLELED SPECTACLE OF WESTERN LIFE AND HISTORY—THE DRAMA OF CIV-ILIZATION.

Swinging spotlights picked out a group of riders in the scenic entrance. They loped across the arena and pulled up under the purple buttes. Then came a file of cowboys, next a band of Mexican vaqueros, last a party of Sioux on shaggy ponies. Buffalo Bill galloped across the field, halting his white horse on hind legs, forefeet in the air. The horse bowed on one knee while Buffalo Bill doffed his hat to a storm of applause.

Now the Drama of Civilization began. Lights came up like sunrise, showing bear, antelope and elk grazing at the edge of a forest. Into the scene trotted two bands of Indians. They joined in a hunting dance, which was ended by the attack of a hostile tribe. The savages fought with bows and arrows, stone hatchets and feather-fringed spears. The lights dimmed on a ground strewn with dying red men.

Then came the first gunfire. On a calico pony Annie Oakley raced around the ring, her pistol shattering targets thrown by Johnny Baker. She leaped to the ground, seized a rifle and broke glass balls in the air. She was all swiftness, grace and magic. When she made her little curtsy and ran from the ring the roof shook with cheers.

The Wild West's first indoor audience had been introduced to the sound of gunfire. The rest of the show would blaze and crackle.

In the next episode a wagon caravan plodded across the prairie. They pulled into a circle for the night camp. It was a peaceful scene until the Indians came whooping.

Another scene showed a cattle ranch with cowboys riding wild horses and roping calves. Up crept the painted savages; they caught the cowboys off guard and helpless. But while they tied their captives, the intent audience heard a distant drumming of hoofbeats. Buffalo Bill and his scouts raced in, and the Indians fled to the Bad Lands.

Johnny Baker, "the Cowboy Kid," did some acrobatic shooting. A Mexican worked rope tricks with a spinning lariat. Across the arena raced the Pony Express; at the relay station the dusty rider leaped onto a fresh horse and pounded away.

While Indian drums drew near, a circle of feathered warriors began to dance. With increasing tempo from the drums they performed the Grass Dance, the Rain Dance, the Antelope Dance and the Buffalo Dance.

A teamster's voice rang out and wagon wheels rumbled. Over a rocky road came the mail from Cheyenne. But bandits lay in ambush. With a rattle of pistol fire they halted the six-mule team. They had surrounded the Deadwood Stage when

Buffalo Bill appeared with rifle blazing. The mail was saved.

The band swung into the marching rhythm of "Garry Owen," the song of Custer's regiment. A floodlight showed the rolling valley of the Little Big Horn. Custer's cavalry appeared, followed by stealthy Indians. With whoops and cries the attack began. Quickly the Indians cut down the doomed troopers. At the end one man was left standing— long-haired General Custer, played by Buck Taylor. He fell under a rain of bullets, and with a whoop of victory the Indians rode away. A swift hoofbeat grew and Buffalo Bill halted a foam- flecked horse. On the screen of mountains, lights spelled out TOO LATE. The great scout bared his head over the body of Custer.

(This drama of Custer's Last Stand was so suc- cessful that it remained in the Wild West per- formance for the next twenty years.)

When the lights came up again the whole company was assembled, with tiny Annie Oakley smiling beside Buffalo Bill. A thunderous applause rolled over the arena. The winter season had a triumphant start.

During that winter the Indians lived in their own camp on Staten Island. Every day they boarded the ferryboat for Twenty-third Street and took the cross-town horsecars to Madison Square. On the way they sat hunched in their bright blankets, staring at the busy streets. When they walked across Fifth Avenue the traffic stopped. The policeman on the corner exchanged greetings with the chiefs from Standing Rock.

"How," he said.

"How," they answered.

Between lines of curious New Yorkers the Indians filed into Madison Square Garden.

That winter the Wild West Show was the talk of the big town. In hotels and restaurants people pointed out the performers.

"There's Buck Taylor, King of the Cowboys, the tall man with long hair."

"That's Johnny Baker, the Cowboy Kid, that nice-looking, round-faced boy."

"There's Annie Oakley—the tiny girl in the small fur hat. Imagine her shooting all those guns."

"There's Buffalo Bill, with his long hair and pointed beard. See the diamond in his neckerchief."

While crowds thronged Madison Square Garden, Nate Salsbury was busy with plans for the future. He talked with shipping men and sent a stream of cable messages to England. In their Staten Island camp the Indians were told about a long journey.

They would go, the interpreter said, across the wide water. They would travel in a big ship, as big as a chief's town. They would come to another country.

At the end of February they held the last performance in Madison Square Garden. Before daybreak the Wild West animals clattered through the New York streets. Horses, mules, steers, buffalo, antelope and elk—their hoofs rattled on the frosty paving stones. They were herded into a cavernous steamship dock on the Hudson River.

"America's National Entertainment" was going to England.

11
Across the Wide Water

The buffalo did not want to go to England. On the steamship dock they tossed their shaggy heads and bellowed. Cowboys lashed them with lariats and prodded them with pitchforks. Still they would not climb the runway to the ship.

At last cargo nets, woven of heavy rope, were spread on the planking, and the animals were lured into them with forkfuls of hay. One at a time the nets swung up, holding a dangling buffalo.

The beasts were lowered like cargo into the forward hatch, where cowboys herded them into a pen.

The other animals clattered up the cleated runway. Horses, mules, steers, elk, antelope—the cowboys kept them moving down the dim 'tweendecks to their stalls.

Wagons, scenery, harness, saddles and the battered stagecoach were loaded. Then a reluctant line filed up the gangway. Red Shirt, Rocky Bear, Little Bull, Cut Meat and Poor Dog led the Indians aboard. They were followed by a superstition. One of their legends said that any Indian who crossed the big water would get sick and die.

At last the gangway swung up and the ship's whistle roared over the harbor. A crowd waved from the dock while the steamer moved away. From the rail the Indians watched the water widen; down in the hold the buffalo bellowed. The cowboy band struck up "The Girl I Left Behind Me." The Wild West was on its way to the Old World.

For the season in England Buffalo Bill had a new title. At Major Burke's suggestion Governor Thayer of Nebraska had made the great plainsman an honorary colonel. He would be Colonel Cody from now on.

No sooner were they out of New York harbor than the ship began to roll in heavy seas. When the captain came down from the navigating bridge the deck was empty. Then he saw Annie Oakley with the salt spray on her face.

"They're all seasick," said the captain. "I saw the Indians close their hatches and the cowboys go below. Then Buffalo Bill disappeared. But you look pleased, Miss Oakley."

Annie Oakley had never been to sea before, but she was a good sailor. For two days she ate alone in the big swaying dining room and walked alone on the pitching deck.

On the third day the wind went down and the ship grew steady. Buffalo Bill appeared, gray as canvas. The Indians stared languidly across the endless water. Some cowboys shuffled into the dining room for a half-hearted meal.

That afternoon Nate Salsbury called the whole company together—Indians, scouts, cowboys, Mexicans, teamsters. There was still a week on the water, he explained, and they must keep their spirits up; he didn't want to arrive in England with a wretched show troop. Every day on shipboard they would put on a show to entertain themselves.

Salsbury began the entertainment with a song and dance from his old "Troubadours" program. Bearded John Nelson and Chief Rocky Bear then talked in sign language about this stormy voyage; their hands heaved and pitched during most of the conversation. Big Jim Kidd gave a demonstration of rope twirling. Mustang Jack, who could leap over a standing horse, now jumped over a piano and back again. Buck Taylor and Tom Clayton gave a knife-throwing exhibition. Johnny Baker and Ben Irving did acrobatic stunts. At the end Annie Oakley neatly lassoed two ship's officers in the doorway. The band played "Oh! Susanna," and the shipboard show was over.

On the twelfth morning the whole show company crowded the rail, watching the shores of England. As they sailed up London River a burst of music came across the water. On a tugboat an English band was playing "The Star-Spangled Banner."

When the ship was moored at Greenwich re-

porters came aboard. They took notes on the som-
breroed Mexicans and the covered wagons. They
watched the cowboys drive stiff-legged steers
and buffalo down the runway. But they were most
interested in the Indians.

To advertise the show Major Burke kept the
star performers in the public view. They visited
Westminster Abbey and the Tower of London.
They attended the Lyceum Theater for a performance of *Faust*. There the Indians sat in front rows,
staring at the stage and eating sugarplums. Buffalo
Bill and Annie Oakley sat in a box.

"That's Miss Oakley, the rider and shootist of
the Wild West Show," people whispered. "Would
you think she could be so small and graceful?"

At Earl's Court in west London hundreds of
workmen were finishing the arena. Its roofed
stands, surrounding a huge oval, seated thirty thousand. Horses, steers and buffalo were browsing
in corrals. The Indians pitched their tepees in a
grove of trees, and the cowboys moved into a big
bunk tent. A lofty screen showing the painted Bad
Lands rose at the end of the arena.

Before the opening performance curious visitors

streamed over the grounds. They admired Annie Oakley's guns and Buffalo Bill's silver-mounted saddle. They wondered at Indian children in buffalo-horn headdresses and at Chief Red Shirt's Sioux war club tied with a horse's tail. They marveled at the long-horned cattle and the shaggy buffalo. It was all strange to them.

One May afternoon a line of gleaming carriages drove into the grand entrance. It was a royal party, headed by the Prince of Wales with his Princess and their wide-eyed children. While Buffalo Bill showed them over the grounds, the Wild West went into action.

The visitors were seated in a box hastily decked with the colors of England and America. For a moment the arena was as empty as a Wyoming valley. Then Annie Oakley galloped past. She snatched a pistol from the ground and shattered flying targets. A herd of buffalo lumbered in, and a hundred savage figures burst out from the Bad Lands. From the distance a herd of steers came charging. Cowboys stampeded them past the royal stand. The Prince of Wales said it was the most exciting show that ever came to England.

Before opening its gates to the public the Wild West gave a command performance for Queen Victoria and her family. Their enthusiasm led to a second performance for the royal guests who were visiting England in celebration of the fiftieth year of the Queen's reign.

For this regal party the Wild West put on a special show. In a quiet interlude a medicine man beat an Indian drum with the leg bone of a turkey and a warrior sang the death chant. *From La-nowa, the windswept tumbling land of the Sioux, the young buck rides away. He makes his campfire in the western sky.*

Crown Prince Edward with four kings from other lands asked to ride in the Deadwood Stage. Buffalo Bill ushered them in and closed the door. A crack of the long whip and the six mules raced away. Above the clatter of hoofs and wheels Utah Frank roared out the old driver's song:

> *Pound 'em on the back,*
> *Let the leaders go;*
> *Never mind the weather*
> *So the wind don't blow.*

When Indians attacked the stagecoach, Buffalo Bill and his cowboys rode to the rescue.

With these performances for royalty the popularity of the Wild West was assured. All summer the crowds kept coming. One London gentleman returned day after day. He attended eighty-six performances.

Annie Oakley was a favorite with English audiences. The newspapers said nothing of her husband, and soon she had suitors. English sportsmen, country gentlemen and college students proposed marriage; she gracefully declined them all. A Welshman who had seen the show a dozen times sent his photograph with an offer of marriage. Annie set the picture on a corral post and put six bullets between the eyes. Then she wrote "Respectfully declined" and mailed it back to Wales.

During the summer Annie Oakley served tea to English mothers and children on the lawn outside her tent. Sometimes she added Indian children to the party—Little Eagle, Seven Up, Little Money. In their buckskin clothing they stared at the starched and ruffled English children, until Annie Oakley put them all at their ease with cakes and lemonade. Before they left, the English visitors looked into a tepee at an Indian baby. It was Chief Red Shirt's tiny son, the first Indian papoose ever born in a foreign land.

After a triumphant year in England the Wild West came home. It was a happy voyage, except for one sadness. Old Charley, Buffalo Bill's favorite hunting horse, died in mid-ocean. Wrapped in canvas and covered with the American flag, he was raised out of the hold. "Old fellow, your journeys are over," said Buffalo Bill. "Willing speed, tireless courage, you have never failed me. If there is a heaven and scouts can enter there, I'll wait at the gate for you, old friend." Then the famous horse was lowered into the gray Atlantic.

In New York harbor a fleet of whistling tugboats came to meet them. Buffalo Bill stood on the captain's bridge. Cowboys and Indians lined the rail. The band played "Yankee Doodle" while the ship came in.

12
Under Paris Skies

The year 1889 was the one hundredth anniversary of the French Republic. To celebrate that national birthday a World's Fair—the *Exposition Universelle*—was held in Paris.

The exposition grounds spread over two hundred acres in the heart of the city. Above its halls and palaces rose the lofty Eiffel Tower. Reaching far above the roofs and domes of Paris, it was the tallest structure in the world.

One of the first visitors to that airy height was

Buffalo Bill. From the observation platform he looked over the great web of Paris. He saw the towers of Notre Dame, the domed Pantheon, and the massive Arc de Triomphe. And he saw something more familiar to him and more surprising to a Frenchman. At the edge of the Parc de Neuilly he saw a camp of Sioux and Pawnee wigwams under the Bad Lands of Dakota.

After just a year at home the Wild West was back in Europe. It had come to France for the great Exposition.

The show grounds spread over thirty acres of fashionable Paris. International visitors wandered through the Indian village and stared at the cardboard buttes. They were puzzled by everything they saw. When the first performance began, the spectators sat silent. They knew nothing of the American frontier. They had never heard of the Pony Express or the Deadwood mail. It was all meaningless to them.

With worried faces Nate Salsbury and Buffalo Bill watched the silent crowd. For the first time the Wild West looked like a complete failure.

Then Annie Oakley began her act. She ran in on twinkling feet and bowed to the silent stands. She raised her gun and broke glass balls in the air. A cowboy loped in, leading a spotted pony. She leaped astride. At a gallop she shattered targets over the rider's head. Back on the ground she threw twin balls into the air and raced to her stand. She jumped the table, seized a gun and whirled while the balls were falling. They vanished in the air.

Twenty thousand Frenchmen could not see her breath coming short and hard. But they saw youth and skill and daring under the mimic mountains. They began to understand the Wild West.

When she bowed again the crowd found its voice. "Bravo! Bravo! *Vive* Annie Oakley!"

The show was launched. By midsummer the Wild West was a Paris frenzy. Fashionable shopkeepers sold Indian blankets, bows and arrows, buffalo robes and bearskins. The famous Rosa Bonheur painted a life-size portrait of Buffalo Bill on horseback. Annie Oakley was made an honorary officer of the French Army.

One of Annie Oakley's admirers was the King of Senegal. He wanted to take her to his home in Africa where she could shoot wild animals in the jungle. To Buffalo Bill he offered a thousand francs for Little Missie. But she was not for sale.

In the fall the show moved on to Spain. They stayed in Spain barely a month, but it seemed endless.

They had just set up in Barcelona when Spanish influenza broke out in the camp. The show was crippled and audiences were small. The doctor carried his black bag into the cowboys' tent and the Indian tepees. The skies hung gray and a chill wind swept the grounds.

On Christmas Day the camp was desolate. Three teamsters were dead of smallpox; ten Indians had died of influenza. In the corral the ponies turned their rumps to the raw December wind. In the wigwams huddled figures chanted the death song of the prairie tribes.

At last they sailed for Italy. In Naples the streets were full of song and laughter and the skies were blue. The show played to noisy crowds, with Mount Vesuvius for a background.

In Rome the cowboys rode wild Italian horses. The show company visited the Vatican and received the Pope's blessing, feathered Indians standing silent under the hand of the Great Medicine. They played to big crowds in Pisa, Bologna, Milan and Verona. In Venice a photographer posed Buffalo Bill and four feathered chiefs in a gondola. That picture appeared in the show programs for many years.

Then came the cities of Austria and Germany. The military Germans admired the Wild West's horsemanship and marksmanship. They also admired the show's organization—the setting up of camp, the packing of equipment, the orderly transportation, the movable kitchens that supplied hot food in all kinds of weather.

In early autumn the Wild West played in historic cities on the Rhine—Düsseldorf, Frankfurt, Cologne. Then in the chill of November they moved on to the old city of Strasbourg. There the long, strenuous season ended and the show went into winter quarters.

It was a gloomy camp. For eighteen months the show had been in foreign lands, in crowded cities, among strange people. The Indians longed for their silent, windswept prairies. The cowboys were restless. Even the steers and buffalo seemed to know they were far from home.

Buffalo Bill had further worries. His European tour had been fully reported in American newspapers, and questions had been raised about the treatment of Indians in the show. Success always invites envy and criticism. Now in Washington, the Indian Commissioner declared that the Indians' place was on their reservation lands, and not on a circus tour of Europe.

United States consuls in Germany were ordered to inspect the Wild West camp. They found the Indians well fed and comfortable. It is true that the Indians wanted to go home, but not because they were mistreated. They were homesick, and Buffalo Bill decided to take them home.

In the quarters near Strasbourg the cowboys and Mexicans settled down for a dull season. Johnny Baker, now a young man of twenty, would be in charge of the winter camp. Annie Oakley and her husband would soon go to England to give shooting exhibitions. Nate Salsbury would go to Belgium,

Germany and Russia, to arrange a schedule for the next summer.

They were all a little homesick while Buffalo Bill and Major Burke went around saying good-bye. The Wild West was a friendly outfit, like a big family. But, like a big family, it sometimes contained rivalries and jealousies. At times Buffalo Bill resented the applause that went to Annie Oakley and the columns the newspapers gave her. But now all resentments were forgotten. The baggage wagon was loading in the chilly dusk. Soon the homeward party would be on their way. Buffalo Bill came to Annie Oakley's tent. Before he left he bent over the autograph book on her table. Afterward she looked at what he had written.

To the loveliest and truest little woman, both in heart and aim, in all the world. Sworn to by and before myself.

W. F. Cody, Buffalo Bill, Strasbourg, 1890.

The next day Buffalo Bill and Major Burke led the Indians aboard a ship at Le Havre. They were excited to be going home. But it was to be a grim winter for them all.

13

Search for Hiding Bill

13
Sunset for Sitting Bull

In the gray November Buffalo Bill and Major Burke arrived in New York with the Wild West Indians. They took them straight to the Indian Bureau at Washington.

Chiefs Rocky Bear and Red Dog spoke for the tribesmen. Through an interpreter they described their travels with the Show and told how they were treated. They made no complaints; they had been well paid, well fed, well cared for. Soon they were on the train for South Dakota.

That winter was a tragic season for the Sioux. Buffalo were gone from the plains and the tribes were confined to reservation lands. Cattle ranchers were stretching barbed-wire fences over their old hunting grounds. In that dark season a frenzy swept the Indian camps; tribal hopes leaped up like smoldering embers catching fire. Sitting Bull foretold the return of the buffalo and the end of the white man's domination. The tribes, he said, would drive out the white intruders and reclaim their hunting lands.

In the reservation camps medicine men stamped all night around the fires, and warriors paraded in their sacred Ghost Shirts. In a swelling chorus the people chanted:

> *The buffalo are coming,*
> *Over the whole earth they are coming,*
> *The buffalo are coming. . . .*

Ranchers and traders up the Missouri told of a sullen gathering of warriors. People remembered

Custer's Massacre. Now they feared an uprising of the tribes.

In that crisis Buffalo Bill offered his service. He was a veteran of the Indian wars. He was a friend of Sitting Bull. All the tribes knew and respected him. Perhaps he could quiet the unrest.

With Major Burke Buffalo Bill hurried to Dakota. When they got off the train at Bismarck they found their old friend Pony Bob Haslam. He said the Indians were in a dangerous mood.

Buffalo Bill looked around at the great bare plains. He had not been in Indian country since Custer's Massacre, in 1876. For years he had enacted the Wild West to the civilized world. Now he was facing the real thing.

At Fort Yates Buffalo Bill hired a wagon and loaded it with gifts for the Indians. In a cold winter daybreak he set out for Sitting Bull's camp. He believed he could persuade Sitting Bull to quiet the angry warriors.

But the army men at Fort Yates resented Buffalo Bill's interference. They saddled their horses and galloped after him. Twenty miles out on the frozen prairie they overtook him and turned him back from his mission.

Meanwhile the Ghost Dance went on in a dozen camps. Restless warriors gathered at Chief Big Foot's village. Others were hurrying to a big camp in the Bad Lands.

In the middle of December a troop of soldiers arrived at Sitting Bull's camp on Grand River. They rode in before daybreak and found the chief asleep in his cabin. He submitted to arrest, but he asked if he could take his favorite horse with him —the horse Buffalo Bill had given him during his season with the Wild West Show.

When the soldiers stepped outside they met an angry circle of warriors. Some of them carried rifles and their faces were painted for the Ghost Dance.

The troops pushed their prisoner forward. Suddenly Sitting Bull gave a cry of resistance— "*Hiyupo! Hopo!*" Guns roared in the cold dawn.

The first to fall was Sitting Bull, with two bullets near his heart.

In the burst of gunfire Sitting Bull's horse began a strange pantomime—bowing, kneeling, lifting his forefeet in a dance. The rattle of rifles had recalled his old show training. He went through his tricks while white and red men fell around him.

(A few months later Buffalo Bill bought the horse from Sitting Bull's people and put him back in the Wild West Show.)

While the soldiers buried Sitting Bull in the frozen prairie, the warriors fled southward to join Big Foot. They told of the death of Sitting Bull and the strange antics of his horse. That, said Chief Big Foot, was a sign that the spirit of Sitting Bull had entered the horse; the old Sioux leader was still among his people.

Big Foot led four hundred Ghost Dancers to the Bad Lands. There they joined the warriors of chiefs Kicking Bear and Short Bull.

Meanwhile army troops were marching to the Bad Lands. They surrounded the Indians at Wounded Knee Creek—a name that would soon become famous in western history.

Chief Big Foot met the soldiers under a white flag of truce. But the troops rolled four cannon onto a ridge, pointing them at the huddled tepees. It was a bitter night, three days before Christmas, with a thin snow flying.

The next morning soldiers went through the camp searching for rifles. A medicine man danced around the Ghost Pole. He shouted to his people in their own tongue, telling them that their sacred Ghost Shirts would turn away the white man's bullets.

Suddenly the medicine man stopped dancing. He scooped up a handful of dirt and threw it in the air.

"*Hoka Hey!*" he cried.

At the sound, some nervous soldiers began shooting. The unarmed Indians were helpless. From the ridge the army cannon poured explosive shells into the camp. Within a few minutes two hundred Indians lay sprawled on the ground.

Then a swirling snowstorm dimmed the battlefield. All day a blizzard raged over the frozen plains.

This was the Battle of Wounded Knee, the last Indian resistance in America.

A week later troops hacked out a huge pit and buried the Indians in a common grave. Then they herded the beaten tribes back to their bleak reservation camps.

According to an old Sioux legend, the south wind blew from the land of death. There was a tenderness in that belief. Sitting Bull and his slain warriors had gone to a country of deep grass and kind skies with a soft wind blowing. They were better off than the survivors.

In the spring of 1891 Buffalo Bill arrived in Philadelphia with a hundred new Indians for the Wild West Show. Two of his chiefs were Short Bull and Kicking Bear. They had been leaders in the Ghost Dance, telling their people that the Sioux nation would be strong and proud again. Now they looked with bewilderment at the strange and powerful world of their conquerors.

With the Indians was an orphan boy who had found a new father and a new name. He was Johnny Burke No Neck.

Major Burke had helped to bury the dead at Wounded Knee. There he found an Indian boy waiting for his father, No Neck, to get up from the frozen ground. Arizona John adopted the boy and brought him to Philadelphia with the other tribesmen. His dark-eyed, solemn picture would soon appear in the programs of the Wild West. He traveled with the show, in Europe and America, for fifteen years.

On a bright day in April, Buffalo Bill and Major Burke and their company of Indians boarded the Steamship *Switzerland*. After a two-weeks' journey they arrived on the Wild West grounds at Strasbourg.

Nate Salsbury, Annie Oakley, Johnny Baker and all the rest were there, ready for the new season's tour. It would take them to Belgium, Holland, Germany, Poland and Russia.

14
At the World's Fair

The most exciting place in the world, during the summer of 1893, was at Jackson Park in Chicago. All day excursion trains hurried along the Lake Michigan shore. At night excursion boats, blazing with lights, passed over the dark water. Day and night people streamed through the gates of the World's Fair on the lake front.

They wandered through vast exhibition halls. They admired the gleaming Court of Honor with

145

its white towers reflected in the water. They wondered at three little ships anchored in the lagoon.

The ships were replicas of the fleet that Columbus had sailed across the unknown Atlantic in 1492. The World's Fair was a celebration, four hundred years later, of the discovery of America.

From the exposition grounds the crowds moved across the street to another wonder. The Wild West Show was there. Every afternoon and evening thousands watched the drama of the American frontier. After three and a half years in Europe the Wild West had come home to America.

Over the Wild West gateway stretched a huge banner. On one side it pictured Columbus on his quarterdeck—PILOT OF THE OCEAN, THE FIRST PIONEER. The other side showed Buffalo Bill on horseback—PILOT OF THE PRAIRIE, THE LAST PIONEER.

The show grounds looked like a western prairie. Inside the gate stood five stuffed buffalo; beyond them were a weathered oxcart and a covered wagon. The crowd moved on to Teddy Roosevelt's log cabin, brought from the Dakota Bad Lands. Over its doorway hung a pair of horns, six feet long, from a Texas steer. Inside a bullet-scarred hut two Indian women sold sweet-grass baskets and beaded moccasins. This was Sitting Bull's cabin, brought all the way from Standing Rock, and the women were his widows.

Visitors to the Indian village could see chiefs straight from frontier history. Rain-in-the-Face, a somber, massive Sioux, was lame from a wound received in Custer's battle. Plenty Horses carried in his body five bullets from the Battle of Wounded Knee. There were a dozen other storied chiefs.

For the World's Fair crowds Buffalo Bill enlarged his company. This season the show included 120 Indians, 75 cowboys, 50 Mexican vaqueros, and scores of horsemen from other countries. The show was called Buffalo Bill's Wild West and Congress of Rough Riders of the World.

In the big arena the cowboy band played "The Star-Spangled Banner." The crowd sat down. The ringmaster's whistle shrilled. Around the track loped Buffalo Bill on a cream-white horse. He was forty-seven, his long hair thinning, his face no longer young. But he still looked imposing on a horse.

His horse bowed to the cheering stands. Then Buffalo Bill's voice boomed: LADIES AND GENTLE-MEN, PERMIT ME TO INTRODUCE TO YOU A CON-GRESS OF ROUGH RIDERS OF THE WORLD.

Out came an American cavalry troop, a squad of British Lancers, a scarlet file of French Chas-seurs, German Uhlans in gleaming helmets, booted Russian Cossacks, white-robed Arab Bedouins, and American cowboys with whirling lariats. These were the world's most daring horsemen. They gal-loped in changing circles, lines and patterns. They formed into a huge revolving wheel. To a final burst of music, under the flags of all nations, they raced off to the wings.

Then the arena was empty except for a single slender rider with a silver star on her upturned hat. Annie Oakley was thirty-three that season, but she looked seventeen. She was all swiftness, grace and magic. She shot on foot, on horseback, from a bicycle. She caught her pony and dashed away.

Following feats of horsemanship, a Sioux hunting party galloped after a herd of buffalo. Then Johnny Baker appeared. He shot flying targets over his shoulder. He shot from behind his back. He shot while standing on his head.

After a broncobreaking contest, the Pony Express raced to the relay station. The Rough Riders jumped their horses over barricades and thrilled the crowd with acrobatic riding. The Deadwood Stage was rescued from painted Indians. Though the program was more varied than before, it was still a drama of western history. The Pony Express, the wagon caravan, the stagecoach, the steers and buffalo, the whooping Indians and reckless cowboys—these belonged to the vanishing frontier, but they would never grow old.

A great cowboy race was held that summer. It began on the Nebraska plains and ended at the gate of the Wild West Show in Chicago. Nine western ranch hands raced for a prize offered by Buffalo Bill.

At the crack of a pistol in the windy little town of Chadron, Nebraska, the nine riders started off.

Among them were Snake Creek Tom, Cockeyed Bill and Rattlesnake Pete. They had a thousand miles to go.

Thirteen mornings later there was a clatter of hoofs outside the show grounds. John Berry on his wiry bronco, Poison, had arrived from the far plains of Nebraska.

When the winner slid down from the saddle, Buffalo Bill shook his hand. They led his tired horse to the stable (where Poison aimed a kick at admiring Major Burke) and took the dusty cowboy to the cook tent for breakfast. The next day in the crowded arena he was awarded the prize.

Autumn brought a haze over Lake Michigan and a chill to the air. On the last day of October the sunset gun boomed over the lake and all the exposition flags came down. The Great World's Fair was over.

For the Wild West it had been a wonderful season. Six million people had passed through the show gates, and distinguished visitors had come from many countries. But now, as the cowboy band played "Home, Sweet Home," there was a touch of sadness in the air. Buffalo Bill was growing old. Nate Salsbury had lost the spring in his step and his beard was turning gray. Annie Oakley, for the first time in her life, felt tired. Even Johnny Baker was glad to think of a quiet winter in Nebraska. And they all wondered—would there ever be another so triumphant season?

15
The Long Show Train

company had to be vaccinated. When their arms swelled and stiffened the Wild West action faltered. In the heat of Custer's battle Indians dropped their rifles and clutched their itching arms.

The route-book of the show tells of accidents that were inevitable in a hard-riding show. An Indian had an arm broken when he was thrown from a bronco. A Mexican was cut when his horse ran against a barbed-wire fence. A cowboy's leg was broken when he was thrown against the corral. One day a cowboy was tossed from "Two Bear Outlaw" and lost his false teeth.

But whether the accidents were grave or trivial, the show went on.

In September, 1896, for the first time the Wild West toured beyond the Mississippi. In October they played at North Platte, where the Old Glory Blowout had been held fourteen years before. Special trains on the Union Pacific brought thousands of people. Buffalo Bill was happy as a boy, and after the show he entertained hundreds of his old friends at Scout's Rest Ranch.

In 1898 the Wild West had a great triumph in Omaha, where it had held its first performance in

1883. Then it was an uncertain venture, with little Johnny Baker following Buffalo Bill around the lot and hoping for a job. Now the Governor of Nebraska and the Mayor of Omaha welcomed the Wild West back. Buffalo Bill made a short speech: "From the Platte to the Danube, from the Tiber to the Clyde, the emblem of Nebraska has always floated over the Wild West."

That was a triumphant day. But a dark day came at the end of the season in 1901.

After a show at Charlotte, North Carolina, the train loaded at midnight—the horses in stock cars behind the locomotive, then the steers and buffalo, then the performers. The long train pulled out and the lights of Charlotte dropped behind. Two hours later came a thunderous crash and the train lurched to a standstill. Above the hissing of steam came the screams of mangled horses.

Red flares showed the wrecked horsecars. "Old Eagle," the star ring horse, was dead. The Deadwood mule team were dead and dying. The bronco "Dynamite" was killed. In the harsh red light cowboys aimed rifles at the wounded and struggling horses.

A figure loomed up beside them. It was Buffalo Bill in his dressing gown, his white hair streaming in the wind, with Johnny Baker beside him. "There's Old Pap," he said, pointing to his white horse in the wreckage. The white head jerked and lifted. He turned to Johnny Baker. "Give me that rifle, son."

In the wreck Annie Oakley was badly injured. After weeks in a hospital she walked with a limp and her hair turned white. She never traveled with the show again.

Nate Salsbury, growing old and frail, retired to a quiet life with his family in New Jersey. There he died on Christmas Eve, 1902, while the Wild West was unloading in England. On the day after Christmas the show opened its London season with flags at half-staff and the cavalry draped with crepe.

This third European tour was less successful than the earlier ones. James A. Bailey, a veteran circus man, had become manager of the show. He painted the wagon wheels, put plumes and spangles on the horses, added a side show full of freaks and marvels. The Wild West was losing its character.

When they returned to America in 1906 Buffalo Bill was aging. Johnny Baker, leaving the shooting and riding to younger men, had become "arenic director." Major Burke kept talking about times past, when Sitting Bull led the buffalo hunt and Annie Oakley thrilled the crowds.

Sometimes Buffalo Bill walked through the grounds at midnight, past the sleeping Indian camp, under the craggy cardboard mountains. A horse whickered at his passing, an old bull buffalo snorted. It was almost like being on the plains again in the years when the West was wild. But that, like the great years of the show, was only memory.

16
End of the Road

In its great years the Wild West Show made millions of dollars for its owners. Yet Buffalo Bill was never a wealthy man. He gave money freely to his relatives and friends. He bought huge tracts of land and left them wild and empty. He invested in unprofitable mines and ranches.

While Nate Salsbury lived, Buffalo Bill had a shrewd and practical business manager. Even James A. Bailey, Salsbury's successor, was an efficient businessman. But in 1907 Bailey died, and there was no experienced manager to take his place. That year the Wild West went into debt. It never prospered again.

After 1900 the Wild West Show had strenuous competition. Big spangled circuses were on the road—Ringling Brothers', Hagenbeck's, and Barnum and Bailey's. They had menageries of wild animals, steam calliopes, clowns, troops of acrobats and aerialists.

But the fatal competition came from a new form of entertainment—the motion picture.

Buffalo Bill had been one of the first figures to appear before the "kinetograph," as the first moving picture camera was called. In 1894, while the show was playing in New York, Buffalo Bill, Annie Oakley and a few Indians gave a brief performance while a photographer cranked the stilted camera. A few weeks later that film was exhibited to a few people in a darkened room on Broadway. Annie Oakley shot some flying targets, Lost Horse stamped out the Buffalo Dance, Buffalo Bill and Iron Tail conversed in sign language. That was the first "western" ever made.

At that time the motion picture was an experiment and a novelty. No one dreamed that every neighborhood, every town and village, would have a moving picture theater.

As the business grew, "western" pictures were most popular. People never tired of seeing Indians, scouts and cowboys on the screen. The early theaters were called "Nickelodeons"—admission five cents. When people all over America could see the moving pictures for a nickel the Wild West Show was doomed.

Buffalo Bill had watched the West change from wilderness to civilization. He saw the telegraph come, then the railroad. He saw the plains fenced with barbed wire and plowed with tractors. He could remember vast herds of buffalo on the open range. One day in 1869 a train on the Kansas Pacific track was stopped for eight hours by the passing of a single rumbling herd. It flowed like a dark river, on and on. Now the country was changed, and even the Wild West Show was "fenced in" by the technical progress of the twentieth century.

But Buffalo Bill did not give up. One of his

old friends was Major Gordon W. Lillie—Pawnee Bill. He had brought the first Indians to Buffalo Bill's show in 1883. Since then Pawnee Bill had developed his own "Far East Show." It was full of wonders from the Orient—Japanese acrobats, Chinese magicians, elephants from Burma and India.

In 1910 the two old friends arranged to combine their shows into a spectacle of THE WILD WEST AND THE FAR EAST. They planned a three-year "farewell tour" which would visit every state in the Union.

The first tour of the combined shows was successful. But the second season brought bad weather and empty stands. Meanwhile the cost of operation went on. They ended the year deep in debt.

Buffalo Bill borrowed money to pay his bills. But the next season was a failure and he could not repay his loan. Gloom lay over the show.

One day in 1913 four men from the sheriff's office came onto the lot in Denver. All the property was seized for debt. Buffalo Bill had given away fortunes in years past. Now no one would help him. The show was slipping from his hands.

On August 21st an auctioneer pounded on a table in the midst of the show grounds. The Wild West was up for sale. To the highest bidder went the broncos, the ring horses, the mustangs, the steers, the buffalo, the wagons, harness, and saddles, the rifles and pistols, the historic old Deadwood Stage.

For years Buffalo Bill had ridden a handsome white stallion, Isham, around the cheering arena. Now he was about to lose his favorite horse. When the bidding ended, Isham was sold to a stranger from Nebraska. The stranger shipped the horse to Buffalo Bill on his new ranch in Wyoming. When the horse arrived, Buffalo Bill was both a happy and a disheartened man. He had his white stallion, but all the rest was gone.

Buffalo Bill was old and tired, but he could not retire. To pay his debts he traveled the next season with the Sells Floto Circus. Too rheumatic to ride horseback, he drove a team of white mustangs in an open buggy. The crowd cheered him, but his heart was heavy.

In 1916 he toured with Miller's 101 Ranch Show. Johnny Baker was with him. This season his contract required him to appear in the saddle. At every performance Johnny Baker helped him up. The old plainsman slumped in the saddle till Johnny said, "Ready, Colonel." Then he straightened and rode into the arena, doffing his hat to the cheering stands. Johnny Baker helped him down.

Buffalo Bill made his last appearance in Portsmouth, Virginia, in November, 1916. Then, tired and ill, he went to his sister's home in Denver. His voice failed. To make his wants known he used the sign language he had learned from the Sioux. He grew weaker and weaker. On a cold January morning in 1917 he died.

For days his body lay in state in a bronze casket under the great dome of the Colorado capitol. Outside stood his horse, Isham, the saddle empty. Thousands filed past the casket. In the balcony a military band played "Tenting on the Old Camp Ground."

That spring a grave was prepared on the top of Lookout Mountain, fifteen miles west of Denver. On the third of June a long procession wound up the mountain road. From the grave they looked over the vast plains, wide as an ocean, where the great scout had roamed. He was buried there while shadows lengthened from the snowy peaks.

From her home at Pinehurst, North Carolina, Annie Oakley sent a farewell tribute. "Goodbye, old friend. The setting sun beyond the western hills will pay daily tribute to the last great pioneer of the West."

Six weeks after Buffalo Bill's burial, Major Burke, his life-long friend, colleague and admirer, died in Washington, D. C.

Annie Oakley lived for ten more years. She died in 1926 near her childhood home in Darke County, Ohio. She was buried in a country cemetery beside a field where she had hunted quail and rabbits in her youth.

Then Johnny Baker was the only one left from the great years of the Wild West. All through Buffalo Bill's show life Johnny Baker was at his side. After his death Johnny Baker was still there. He stayed on Lookout Mountain as custodian of his hero's grave.

There he built a museum, "Pahaska Tepee." He filled it with relics of Buffalo Bill—his rifles, revolvers and saddles, his pictures and show posters.

Thousands of people drove up the mountain to see Buffalo Bill's grave. They lingered in Pahaska Tepee, admiring the old scout's relics and looking from its observation porch over the panorama of the plains.

As the years passed Johnny Baker became a weathered man with distant eyes and distant memories. He told visitors about his boyhood in Nebraska, his first job with Buffalo Bill and his travels with the Wild West for thirty years. Sometimes he showed them his gold watch, inscribed:

Presented to Johnny Baker
Champion Boy Shot of the World
by his guardian
William F. Cody
Aug. 18, 1886

Johnny Baker watched over Buffalo Bill's grave while he himself grew old and tired. He died in Denver in 1931, the last survivor of the great Wild West Show.

Epilogue:
The Show Goes On

Cody, Wyoming, is a town of just two thousand, but every year it has hundreds of thousands of visitors. Many of them are on their way to Yellowstone National Park, and most of them stop in Cody at a low log building which looks like a frontier lodge. It is the Buffalo Bill Museum, containing hundreds of souvenirs of the great showman's life.

Buffalo Bill founded the town and gave it his

name. With profits from the Wild West Show he bought his big T E Ranch outside of Cody. When he acquired it, it was a windswept empty range, without cattle or horses and without a name. At Deadwood, in the Black Hills, he bought a string of horses from his old friend Mike Russell. Cody and his cowboys trailed five hundred horses, all bearing Russell's E brand, over the Big Horn Mountains. Instead of re-branding all those horses, Buffalo Bill took over the T E brand and gave that name to his new ranch.

To the Museum visitors Buffalo Bill is more than a great showman and a historic plainsman. He is a symbol of American pioneering. He is a personification of the Old West.

After looking at pictures and posters, the saddles, guns and blankets, visitors go to a dusty field beyond the Museum. There, every day in the summer season the T E ranch hands hold a rodeo. They ride broncos and rope cattle. They rescue a stagecoach from attacking bandits.

The Museum is a silent place, full of mute reminders of the vanished West. But the arena is full of whoops and cries and the pound of flying hoofs. There the Old West comes to life again.

Every year rodeos are held in the western towns, and rodeo troops travel to county fairs and state fairs across the country. Each winter the top hands compete in a big rodeo in Madison Square Garden in New York.

So the Wild West Show goes on. Buffalo Bill, Sitting Bull, Annie Oakley and Johnny Baker are gone. The West has changed, and big combines harvest wheat on the old buffalo plains. But the legend and history of the West are not forgotten. In western stories, in moving pictures, in radio and television programs, the Old West lives on. And in every rodeo the rattle of hoofs and the creak of leather are echoes from the great Wild West Show.

INDEX

American Horse, Chief, 84, 95
"Annie Oakley Day," 99

Bailey, James A., 158, 163-64
Baker, Johnny, 7-10, 79, 84, 151
  and Annie Oakley, 42-44, 73,
    75, 106
  as "arenic director," 159
  and Buffalo Bill, 18, 20-21, 65-
    66, 86, 157, 167-69
  death of, 170
  at Madison Square Garden,
    106-07, 109
  museum built by, 169
  on ship bound for Europe, 116
  in Wild West Show, 15, 18,
    20-21, 26, 106-07, 109, 130,
    142, 149
  at World's Fair, Chicago, 149
  and wreck at Charlotte, 158
Baker, Lew, 8
Barnum, P. T., 97
Bates, Sergeant, 85
Battle of Wounded Knee, 140
Bean, Dick, 84
Beecher, Henry Ward, 104
Berry, John, 150
Big Foot, Chief, 138-39
Bogardus, A. H., 26, 32
Bonheur, Rosa, 127
Boston, Wild West Show in, 21,
    26, 72-75
Brooklyn, Wild West Show in,
    21, 155

Buffalo, in Wild West Show, 13,
    19, 30, 117-18
  reluctant to board ship, 113
Buffalo Bill, 5-10, 41, 43-46, 72,
    74, 79, 86, 128, 141-42, 156
  aging of, 150-51, 159
  ankle injury of, 85
  and Baker, Johnny, 18, 20-21,
    65-66, 86, 157, 167-69
  Cody founded by, 173
  as colonel, 115
  on Custer, 65
  death of, 168
  on death of favorite horse, 121
  debts of, 166-67
  and Edison, 96
  in England, 117-18
  European worries of, 130
  grave of, 168-70
  at Indian Bureau, 135
  on Indians, 64-65
  last appearance of, 168
  at Madison Square Garden,
    104-09
  mansion of, at North Platte,
    83
  with Miller's 101 Ranch Show,
    167
  in motion picture, 164
  on Oakley, Annie, 131
  in Paris, 126-27
  portrait of, 127
  and Salsbury, 22, 25, 77
  seasickness of, 115
  with Sells Floto Circus, 167

177